THE LEGAL RIGHTS
OF THE ELDERLY

Practising Law Institute Guides

ESTATE PLANNING
How to Preserve Your Estate for Your Loved Ones
by Jerome A. Manning

INVESTOR'S RIGHTS HANDBOOK
• *Stocks* • *Bonds* • *Mutual Funds*
•*Other Securities Investments*
by Larry D. Soderquist

YOUR RIGHTS IN THE WORKPLACE
Everything Employees Need to Know
by Henry H. Perritt, Jr.

PERSONAL BANKRUPTCY
What Every Debtor and Creditor Needs to Know
SECOND EDITION
by William C. Hillman

A Practising Law Institute Guide

THE LEGAL RIGHTS OF THE ELDERLY

Sia Arnason
Ellen Rosenzweig
Andrew Koski

Practising Law Institute
New York City

Distributed to the trade by Publishers Group West.

ISBN: 0-87224-079-7
Library of Congress catalog card number: 95-69568

Contents

The Legal Rights for the Elderly

Table of Contents

vii

What are the SSI limits on resources? 30
What exactly is meant by "resources"? 30
Can I own a home or other property and still be
    eligible for SSI? 30
How is other real estate treated? 31
Is a joint bank account counted towards the resource limit? ... 31
How are trusts treated for SSI purposes? 32
Are life insurance policies considered when applying for SSI? .. 32
Can I dispose of my savings in order to become
    eligible for SSI? 33

OTHER ELIGIBILITY ISSUES 33
Are there citizenship requirements to become eligible for SSI? . 33
Are there residency requirements to become eligible for SSI? .. 34
If I live with another person, or in a group home, will my SSI
    be affected? 34
How will a hospitalization affect my SSI benefits? 35
How can I pay for my housing if I have only $30 a month? 35
Can children be eligible for SSI? 35
Can a person whose spouse is not eligible for SSI be eligible? .. 36

APPLYING FOR BENEFITS 36
Where do I apply for SSI? 36
What documents do I need to apply for SSI? 36

CHANGES IN BENEFITS AND PERSONAL CIRCUMSTANCES 37
Will my SSI benefit stay the same each year? 37
Once eligible for SSI, will I receive benefits forever? 37
What changes in circumstances have to be reported to the
    Social Security Administration? 38
What if I become unable to manage my own SSI income? 38
Should the Social Security Administration be notified of the
    death of an SSI beneficiary? 39

APPEALS, INCLUDING APPEALS OF OVERPAYMENTS 39
What can I do if my application for SSI is denied? 39
Can I appeal other Social Security Administration decisions
    about my SSI benefits? 40
What is meant by an "overpayment"? 40

Table of Contents

Table of Contents

The Legal Rights for the Elderly

Table of Contents

Table of Contents

Table of Contents

Table of Contents

Table of Contents

Table of Contents

Table of Contents

Acknowledgments

This book could not have been written without the help of many friends. Among those who made it possible for us to research the answers to the questions raised in this book are the Brookdale Foundation, a major supporter of the Institute on Law of the Brookdale Center on Aging of Hunter College; the UJA—Federation of Jewish Philanthropies, which has supported our Entitlements Advocacy for the Frail Elderly Project; the Interest on Lawyer Account (IOLA) Fund of New York State, which has supported the Harlem Entitlements Legal Project; and the Isaac H. Tuttle Fund, which has given its generous support to this particular book.

We are also indebted to the following friends who allowed us to include some of their own publications or to base parts of this book on material they have prepared: Karen Kaplan, Ann Fade, and Mary Meyer of Choice in Dying, Inc., for inclusion of the material on advance directives; Jean Murphy and Judith Kahn of Friends and Relatives of Institutionalized Aged, Inc. in New York City, for materials collected for the chapter on nursing home care; and Charlie Sabatino of the American Bar Association's Commission on Legal Problems of the Elderly for permission to include the Model Statement of Home Care Client Rights and Responsibilities. We also wish to thank Jill Ann Boskey, Managing Attorney of MFY Legal Services SSI/ SSD Project; Barbara Samuels, Staff Attorney for Brooklyn Legal Services Corporation; and Louise M. Tarantino, Staff Attorney of the Greater Upstate Law Project, who gave us valuable comments and suggestions.

Finally, we are most grateful to Sam Sadin, Rick Moody, and Rose Dobrof of the Brookdale Center on Aging, who have challenged us for many years and without whom this book would never have been written; and we thank the administrative staff of the Institute on Law, Paul Fleischmann and Vernon Jefferson, who helped with word processing and the assembling of the chapter on resources.

Introduction

The scope and variety of assistance programs currently available to elderly or disabled Americans is mind-boggling. In 1994, an estimated 43 million Americans were receiving Social Security or Supplemental Security Income benefits. Millions are also eligible for Medicare, Medicaid, and other entitlement programs.

Knowing what's available to you and actually achieving assistance can be a long and thankless process. Qualification requirements and application procedures are often buried in thick government manuals or hard-to-read agency publications.

That's why *The Legal Rights of the Elderly* was created. It pulls together in one place a complete description of the full range of assistance programs available to you — with the information you need to successfully apply for and receive all the benefits to which you're entitled.

In an easy-to-read question-and-answer format, *The Legal Rights of the Elderly* takes the mystery out of qualifying for and obtaining the assistance. There's a chapter on each major program, spelling out what the benefits are, who's entitled to them, and how to deal successfully with the governing body or agency.

Chapter 1 focuses on old age benefits under the Social Security program, the cornerstone of income assurance for older or disabled Americans. You'll find a complete explanation of what the benefits are for the insured, their dependents, and their survivors, how to qualify, and even how to appeal if benefits are denied.

Chapter 2 covers Supplemental Security Income (SSI), the safety net designed to meet the ordinary living expenses of people with incomes below the poverty level.

Chapter 3 deals with the substantial disability benefits available under both Social Security and SSI, including the complex and tricky requirements for establishing medical and functional disability. (Persistence can pay off: more than half of all denied applications have been successfully appealed.)

Chapter 4 describes the many income, health care, disability, educational, home financing, and other benefits available to veterans, their dependents, and their survivors.

Chapter 5 focuses on Medicare, the nation's most important health insurance program for the elderly, and covers eligibility requirements of Parts A and B, benefits of both parts, as well as administrative and appeals procedures.

Chapter 6 covers Medicaid, the "needs-based" medical assistance program for Americans with very limited savings and low incomes. Chapter 7 describes alternatives for Supplemental Medical Insurance to close the gaps in Medicare coverage.

Chapters 8 and 9 deal with long-term care, starting with the variety of home care and community-based services available to elderly Americans (chapter 8) and funding sources for nursing home care (chapter 9), should this become a necessity.

Chapter 10 discusses the importance of lifetime planning, with step-by-step guidance on how to give a trusted relative or friend legal authority to handle your financial or personal affairs, in the event you become incapacitated.

Chapter 11 provides an invaluable listing of nearly 500 agencies and other groups available to help you, with contact addresses and phone numbers for more information.

How to Use This Book

This book's organization, question-and-answer format, and multiple finding aids make it easy to use in a number of ways. Here are just some of them.

1. Read the brief chapter introductions to zero in on the programs that are applicable to your situation.
2. Use the time-saving questions (in heavier type within each chapter) to get detailed information on benefits, qualification and application procedures.
3. Get the contact information you need to proceed with your application in chapter 11.
4. Refer to the index at the back of the book or the detailed table of contents at the front to get quick answers to specific questions.
5. Skim the discussions of benefits within each chapter to be sure you're getting all the assistance to which you're entitled.

Why This Book Was Written

The authors have long been involved in counseling elderly and disabled Americans in obtaining needed assistance. Affiliated with the Institute on Law and Rights of Older Adults, they are part of the author team that produces the *New York Elder Law Handbook*, the definitive guide for lawyers, health care professionals, social workers, financial planners, and other advocates for New York State's elderly.

They saw a clear need for an in-depth, readable reference for the population they serve — a plain-English guide to the full range of assistance programs available, with expert advice on how to seek and obtain needed benefits.

If you're a disabled or elderly American, or a family member or friend, you'll find *The Legal Rights of the Elderly* an indispensable guide.

1

Old Age Benefits Under Social Security

Qualifying for Benefits . . . Old Age Benefits . . . Spouses' Benefits . . . Children's Benefits . . . Survivors' Benefits . . . Death Benefits . . . Applying for Benefits . . . Representative Payees . . . Appeals.

The Social Security program, more formally known as the Old Age, Survivors, and Disability Insurance (OASDI) program, is administered by the federal government through local District Offices of the Social Security Administration.

Social Security is the cornerstone of income for older Americans and is best known for its retirement benefit program. Over 90 percent of older Americans report receiving benefits from Social Security. The program is, however, much more than a retirement program. It also offers disability benefits for disabled workers, benefits to children and other dependents, and benefits to survivors of people who have reached so-called "insured status."

The Social Security program is "insurance based." That is, benefits are based on taxes withheld from earnings and matched by employers throughout the employment history of individual workers. As the American Association of Retired Persons (AARP) points out, Social Security benefits are not to be confused with charity or welfare benefits; they are an "earned right" and are designed to replace income lost due to the retirement, disability, or death of a worker. Generally speaking, the more workers pay into the system, the more they are likely to get back from it. Individual benefits are calculated through a complex formula that includes consideration of the amount of time a worker has actually contributed taxes to the system, the worker's age at the time benefits are applied for, the amount of the worker's total earnings, and the type of benefit for which an application is made.

The Social Security OASDI program provides five kinds of benefits, available to people who have achieved "insured status," their dependents, their survivors, and the disabled. An overview of those benefits is found in table 1-1. This chapter describes the old age benefits program, including benefits for dependents and survivors and death benefits. Disability benefits under the Social Security Program are described in chapter 3.

TABLE 1-1
FIVE SOCIAL SECURITY BENEFITS

Type of benefit	Beneficiaries
Old age benefit	• people age 62 or older
Disability benefits	• disabled workers of any age
Dependent benefits	• spouses 62 or older • spouses of any age who are caring for (1) a child under 16 or (2) a disabled child of any age • divorced spouses • dependent, unmarried children under 18 (19 if full-time students) • disabled, unmarried children 18 and older
Survivor benefits	• widow(er)s 60 or older • widow(er)s of any age who are caring for (1) a child under 16 or (2) a disabled child of any age • divorced surviving spouses • disabled widow(er)s between 50 and 60 • dependent, unmarried children under 18 (19 if full-time students) • disabled children over 18 • dependent parents of deceased worker
Lump sum death benefits	• widow(er)s of deceased worker • dependent children who were receiving benefits at time of worker's death

QUALIFYING FOR BENEFITS

How do I qualify for Social Security benefits?

Your earnings record is the key to determining whether
you have attained "insured status" and are entitled to
benefits. Your earnings record takes into account the
length of time you have been employed and the amount
of your earnings during that time. It is based on the
number of "quarters of coverage" you have earned.

What is meant by a "quarter of coverage"?

In order to meet the quarter of coverage test, you have to
earn a minimum amount in a quarter. In 1995, a worker
was credited with a quarter of coverage if he or she had
earned at least $630 in that quarter of the year. You can
be credited with a maximum of four quarters of coverage
during a year.

For example, Mrs. Jones earned $2,000 during 1995.
She therefore receives credit for three quarters of coverage (3 x $630 = $1,890; the additional $110 is disre-
garded). In order to be credited with four quarters of
coverage for the year, Mrs. Jones would have to have
earned at least $2,520 (4 x $630) in 1995.

What is "insured status"?

The Social Security Administration determines insured
status through different formulas, which depend on the
type of benefit you are applying for. Insured status also
determines whether dependent, survivor, or death benefits will be available to your family members. There are
basically three different types of insured status:

(1) fully insured status for old age benefits;

(2) insured status for disability benefits; and

(3) currently insured status.

Since this chapter focuses on old age benefits, the most important status here is "fully insured."

How can I achieve fully insured status for old age benefits?

In general, forty quarters of coverage will fully insure any worker who reaches 62 years of age during or after 1991. For those who became 62 before 1991, fewer quarters of coverage are needed to reach fully insured status (see table 1-2).

TABLE 1-2
QUARTERS OF COVERAGE REQUIRED
FOR FULLY INSURED STATUS

Year of birth	Quarters of coverage needed
1922	33
1923	34
1924	35
1925	36
1926	37
1927	38
1928	39
after 1928	40

How can I achieve insured status for disability benefits?

The number of quarters of coverage needed to achieve insured status for disability benefits is different from the number of quarters of coverage needed for retirement benefits and depends on the age of the disabled worker. See chapter 3 for details on Social Security disability benefits.

Is it possible to obtain Social Security benefits if the worker does not meet the required insured status for old age or disability benefits?

Yes, survivors of deceased workers may be eligible for some Social Security benefits under the so-called currently insured status. To be currently insured, the deceased worker would have to have worked six quarters out of the thirteen quarters immediately preceding the worker's death.

People who think they may fall into this category should contact their local Social Security District Office immediately.

OLD AGE BENEFITS

At what age do old age benefits begin?

Most people are under the impression that Social Security old age benefits start at age 65. However, this is a misconception. If you are otherwise eligible, you can start receiving old age benefits at age 62. But when you start your benefits at age 62, your monthly checks will be less than you would have received if you had waited until you were 65. Full Social Security benefits can be obtained only if you begin taking them at age 65; while increased Social Security benefits can be obtained if you continue to work beyond age 65 and apply for your benefits at some later date.

How much are my benefits reduced if I retire at age 62?

A sixty-two-year-old person who is fully insured, retires early, and immediately applies for old age benefits will receive 80 percent of the amount of the benefits he or she would have been eligible for at age 65. Once benefits are reduced, they will remain so for the rest of the worker's life.

How much are benefits increased if I delay retirement and continue to work?

You earn "delayed retirement credits" for each month that you work, without receiving Social Security benefits, after age 65.

Persons who have reached fully insured status and decide to delay receiving Social Security benefits until after age 65 can still apply for Medicare benefits at age 65 while they are employed. See chapter 5.

Can I work and also receive Social Security old age benefits at the same time?

Yes, Social Security recipients may work while they receive old age benefits. However, benefits will be reduced for people between ages 62 and 70 if their annual earnings exceed a certain amount. The reduction of benefits depends on the age of the Social Security recipient and

The Legal Rights of the Elderly

the amount earned. The limit on the amount of earnings before reductions are made is revised each year by the Social Security Administration. Table 1-3 indicates the earnings limits for 1995.

TABLE 1-3
EARNINGS LIMITS FOR
SOCIAL SECURITY BENEFICIARIES, 1995

Age of beneficiary	Amount earned*	Reduction
under 65	over $8,160	$1 for every $2 earned
65 through 69	over $11,280	$1 for every $3 earned
70 and older	—	no reduction regardless of amount earned

*For the purpose of this table, "earnings" is defined as gross income from wages and net income from self-employment. Dividends, interest on bank accounts, and payments from a pension are not considered earnings for this purpose and will not reduce Social Security benefits.

Does one pay taxes on old age benefits?

Most Social Security beneficiaries (about 80 percent) do not pay taxes on their old age benefits. However, some people with high incomes from Social Security and other sources may have to pay taxes on their Social Security income. Whether your benefits are subject to tax depends

8

on your filing status and your total annual income (see Table 1-4). The Social Security Administration sends its beneficiaries annual Social Security Benefit Statements (Form SSA-1099) in January of each year to inform them of their individual Social Security income for the previous year.

TABLE 1-4
TAXATION OF SOCIAL SECURITY BENEFITS

Filing status	Annual income*	Percent of Social Security benefits taxed
Single	up to $24,999	no tax on benefits
	$25,000 - $33,999	50% of benefits
	$34,000 and over	85% of benefits
Married filing jointly	up to $31,999	no tax on benefits
	$32,000-$43,999	50% of benefits
	$44,000 and over	85% of benefits

*In this table, "income" is defined under IRS rules as one-half your Social Security benefits, plus your other taxable income, plus your tax-exempt interest income, less adjustments to income such as alimony and contributions to IRAs and Keoghs.

Is there a lifetime maximum amount one can receive from Social Security?

No, there is no such limit. Regardless of how long you live, you can continue to receive benefits. Your monthly amount of Social Security benefits will remain the same, except for annual cost of living increases.

How are Social Security benefits computed?

The Social Security Administration computes your benefits through a fairly complex formula, based on the number of credited quarters of coverage; the amount of earnings; and your age at the time of retirement, disability, or death. Through this formula a base benefit is established for you, called the Primary Insurance Amount (PIA). The PIA is based on your taxable earnings averaged over a lifetime of employment and converted to a monthly figure. For people who became eligible after 1978, the average monthly earnings are also indexed to adjust for the differences of the dollar's purchasing power over time (annual wages of $10,000 in 1970 were worth far more in 1970 than annual wages of $10,000 in 1994).

Is the PIA the exact amount I will receive?

No, the PIA is not necessarily the same as the Social Security benefit you might receive. The PIA is the base amount that a fully insured worker would receive if he or she retired at age 65. As was pointed out before, in addition to a person's lifetime earnings, other factors are also taken into account to arrive at the actual amount of benefits a person will receive. These factors include the age of the worker at the time of retirement, onset of disability, or death, and whether the worker continues to work while receiving benefits. Since dependents' and survivors' benefits are a percentage of the worker's benefits, the PIA amount is also used to determine the family maximum benefit amount and the individual shares of the family maximum that individual dependents or survivors may receive.

What is meant by a "family maximum benefit" and how does it affect my benefits and those for my dependents or survivors?

There is a maximum family benefit that all of your dependents and/or survivors can qualify for in addition to what you might receive. The total amount payable on one worker's credit cannot exceed 150 percent to 188 percent of the worker's PIA, depending on its size.

Regardless of how many dependents share in the maximum family benefit, the retired worker will always receive the full amount of benefits for which he or she is eligible.

Is it possible to obtain an estimate of my PIA ahead of time?

Yes, you can request a copy of your earnings record and the estimated amount of your PIA by calling the Social Security Administration at 1-800-772-1213 or by going to your local Social Security District Office and asking for Form 7004-SM, "Request for Earnings and Benefit Estimate Statement."

In order to ensure that all of your earnings are credited properly, the Social Security Administration advises that you request an Earnings and Benefit Estimate Statement every three years. This makes it easier to correct any errors and increases the likelihood that evidence will be available to support your claim that an error was made.

SPOUSES' BENEFITS

Is the spouse of a retired or disabled Social Security beneficiary eligible for Social Security benefits?

Yes. As table 1-5 indicates, the wife or husband of a retired or disabled worker who receives Social Security benefits can get a benefit up to 50 percent of the worker's PIA while the worker is still alive (benefits for spouses age 62 to 64 are proportionately reduced). However, certain conditions have to be met:

* the worker is receiving old age or disability benefits;
* the couple have been married at least one year; or if not married, they are the natural parents of a child;

TABLE 1-5
BENEFITS FOR SPOUSES

Beneficiary	% of worker's PIA
Spouse, age 65	50
Spouse, age 62	37.5
Spouse, any age, caring for minor or disabled child	50

- the spouse is at least 62 years old; or the spouse (of any age) cares for a child under the age of 16 or a disabled child; and
- the spouse is not entitled to an old age or disability income, based on his or her own work record, that is equal to or more than the retired or disabled worker's PIA.

Is the divorced spouse of a Social Security beneficiary eligible for these benefits?

Yes, divorced spouses are eligible for spouses' benefits if certain conditions are met:

- the couple was married at least ten years;
- the worker on whose credit benefits are to be collected is insured, and is either disabled or at least 62 years old (the worker does *not* have to be receiving Social Security benefits);
- the divorced spouse is not married;
- the divorced spouse is at least 62 years old; and
- the couple must have been divorced at least two years.

There is an exception: since 1991, spouse's benefits are also available to divorced spouses who do not meet the duration of marriage requirement if both spouses were receiving retirement benefits prior to the divorce.

Can current spouses and former (divorced) spouses of retired or disabled workers receive benefits simultaneously?

Yes, more than one person can receive spouse's benefits on the basis of a retired or disabled worker's record. However, individual benefits for dependents and survivors are reduced when there are two or more dependents or survivors receiving benefits.

What happens if the spouse is eligible for Social Security on his or her own record?

In general, spouses who are entitled to Social Security benefits, based on their own employment history, receive whichever amount is larger, that is, Social Security benefits based on their own PIA or 50 percent of their spouse's benefits.

Is it true that marriage will reduce people's old age benefits?

Not necessarily. People who plan to marry and who each have Social Security old age income, based on their own work history, will not be negatively affected by their subsequent marriage. However, if you had Social Security benefits based on the work history of a former spouse, a subsequent marriage would cause you to lose your spouse's benefits from your first marriage (which may be higher than the benefits you might be entitled to under your second marriage).

CHILDREN'S BENEFITS

Are children eligible for benefits on the basis of a retired, disabled, or deceased parent's PIA?

Yes, any unmarried children under the age of 18 (or under age 19 if they are students in an elementary or secondary school) who are dependent on a retired, disabled, or deceased worker are eligible to receive dependents' benefits until their eighteenth (or nineteenth) birthday. Dependent children of a retired or disabled worker can receive up to 50 percent of the retired or disabled worker's PIA. Dependent children of a deceased worker can receive up to 75 percent of the deceased parent's PIA. In addition, disabled dependent children who became totally disabled before the age of 22 can obtain dependents' benefits for as long as their own disability lasts.

Which children will qualify for dependents' benefits?

The Social Security Administration provides dependents' benefits to all children who are dependent on the retired, disabled, or deceased worker, including:

- natural children;
- illegitimate children with inheritance rights;
- legally adopted children;
- equitably adopted children (that is, children whose adoptive parent died before the adoption process was completed);
- stepchildren who have been stepchildren for one year or more;
- grandchildren (under certain conditions) whom the worker has adopted or has been supporting (for instance, when the child's parents are disabled or deceased); and
- stepgrandchildren (under certain conditions).

How is "dependency" established?

In order to establish dependency, it is necessary to document that the child lives with the worker and that the worker contributes substantially to the child's support.

SURVIVORS' BENEFITS

Are widows and widowers eligible for Social Security benefits?

Yes, a worker's widow(er) who is 65 years or older can get a survivor's benefit that is equal to 100 percent of the deceased worker's PIA. Widow(er)s who are less than 65 years of age can obtain a percentage of the deceased worker's full benefits (see table 1-6). If the widow(er) is disabled, he or she can obtain survivor's benefits at age 50, and if the widow(er) is taking care of a child under age 16, he or she can obtain so-called mother's (or father's) benefits at any age.

Are divorced people eligible for survivor's benefits?

Yes, divorced widow(er)s are able to obtain benefits on the deceased worker's credit. However, certain conditions have to be met:
- the marriage has to have lasted at least ten years;
- the surviving divorced widow(er) is at least 60 years old or at least 50 years old if disabled; and
- the survivor is not entitled to an old age benefit that is equal to or more than the deceased worker's PIA.

Are the parents of a deceased worker eligible for Social Security benefits?

Yes, a *dependent* parent of a deceased worker is eligible for survivors' benefits if the following conditions are met:
- the worker was fully insured at the time of death;
- the parent is not entitled to an old age benefit that is equal to or more than the parent's benefit available under the worker's credit; and

16

- the parent was receiving at least one-half support from the worker at the time the worker died or at the onset of the worker's disability, if the disability lasted until the worker's death.

TABLE 1-6

SURVIVORS' BENEFITS*

Beneficiary	% of deceased worker's PIA
Widow, age 65	100
Widow, age 62	82.5
Widow, age 60	71.5
Disabled widow, age 50	71.5
Widow, any age, with child under 16	75
Surviving child	75
Surviving dependent parent	82.5

*Note that if there are several dependents or survivors entitled to support, the amount available to each person will be less than the percentages of the worker's PIA shown in the table above. For example, if the worker is survived by two dependent parents, each will receive 75 percent of the worker's PIA.

DEATH BENEFITS

Who is entitled to receive death benefits?

One lump sum death benefit of $255 is available on the credit of a fully insured or currently insured deceased worker. This death benefit can be paid to:

- the deceased worker's widow(er) who was living with the worker at the time of death; or
- the widow(er), not living with the worker at the time of death, who was eligible for the worker's survivor's or mother's or father's benefit in the month of the worker's death; or
- if there is no surviving widow(er), a surviving child who was eligible for dependent's benefits in the month that the worker died.

Applications to receive death benefits must be filed at the local District Office within two years of the worker's death.

APPLYING FOR BENEFITS

How do I apply for old age benefits?

To obtain Social Security benefits, you have to submit an application to the Social Security Administration. Applications for old age benefits (and for all other types of Social Security benefits as well) are filed at the local District Offices of the Social Security Administration. Applications can be requested and completed by phone or in person, but they won't be filed until you have signed the application form.

When should I apply for old age benefits?

It is usually advisable to start the application process several months before you actually want to receive benefits, since the whole process may take some time. If you meet the eligibility requirements as of the day of the application, you will receive retroactive benefits to the date of the application.

Are applications for disability, dependents', or survivors' benefits handled the same way?

Yes, all applications are started at the District Offices. However, disability, dependents', or survivors' benefits require documentation and verification of the applicant's disability, dependent, or survivor status. The process can therefore take substantially longer than applying for old age benefits. The Social Security Administration issues retroactive checks if the applicant is found to have been eligible for the benefit at the time he or she applied.

Is it possible to have a check directly deposited in a checking account?

Yes, the Social Security Administration provides for direct deposit of checks. Applications for direct deposit of checks can be made at the local District Office or by calling 1-800-772-1213.

What if my Social Security check is lost or stolen?

If a monthly check is lost or stolen, the Social Security Administration will issue a new check to the rightful beneficiary. Applications for a replacement are made at the local District Office.

REPRESENTATIVE PAYEES

Is it possible for another person to receive a Social Security check on behalf of a Social Security beneficiary?

Yes, in certain circumstances, if the beneficiary is not able to manage his or her own income, another person can be authorized by the Social Security Administration to receive the Social Security check on behalf of the beneficiary. A person who receives a Social Security check on behalf of a Social Security beneficiary is called a "representative payee."

How is a representative payee appointed?

In order for someone to be appointed representative payee, an application must be filed at the local District Office and a medical form must be completed by the beneficiary's doctor, indicating that there are medical reasons for the person's inability to manage his or her income. Common reasons are advanced chronic illness (such as Alzheimer's disease), mental illness, alcoholism, and drug abuse.

Who can serve as a representative payee?

A family member or friend can be a representative payee; so can certain agencies and institutions. The Social Security Administration tries to find someone who is in a position to know of and look after the needs of the beneficiary.

Can a representative payee be appointed against the wishes of the beneficiary?

Yes. But the beneficiary is entitled to advance notice of the appointment, and he or she has the right to appeal. An appeal might challenge the decision that an appointment of a representative payee is necessary or the choice of a particular person as payee. (Appeals are discussed below.)

What is the obligation of a representative payee?

Once the Social Security check (or Supplemental Security Income check) is received by the representative payee, he or she is obligated to pay the beneficiary's monthly expenses for housing, food, clothing, and similar needs, to ensure that the person is cared for adequately. The representative payee must also prepare an annual accounting and submit it to the Social Security Administration for review.

Is a representative payee also able to manage other funds of the beneficiary, such as pension income or savings accounts?

No. The authority of a representative payee is limited. The representative payee gains access only to the Social Security income of the beneficiary. Thus, if the beneficiary needs other sources of income during any given month, other financial management arrangements may have to be considered, such as guardianship. See chapter 10.

APPEALS

Is it possible to appeal a decision made by the Social Security Administration?

Yes, there is a multi-step administrative appeal process you can use if you are not satisfied with a decision made by the Social Security Administration. But you are subject to time limits for appeals. So if you think that the wrong decision has been made in your case, you should contact the nearest Social Security District Office immediately and request a so-called reconsideration of the decision.

What are the steps in the appeals process?

Step one is the reconsideration, when your claim is reviewed by someone in the Social Security Administration who has not been involved before. This step usually involves a review of your entire case file. In order to help the Social Security Administration, it is very important to submit any additional documentation that may clarify the issue. If the decision after reconsideration is again negative, you may go to the second step in the appeal process.

Step two is an Administrative Law Judge Hearing. This is a very important part of the process, because you have the right to appear before an administrative law judge (ALJ) and testify in person. You have other rights as well: they include the right to read the files of the Social Security Administration prior to the hearing; to bring witnesses; to bring additional evidence and documentation; and to subpoena and cross-examine witnesses. In most instances, the ALJ hearing will be the end of the appeal;

however, if the hearing decision is again negative and you feel that you have a valid claim, you may be able to go to the next step.

Step three in the appeals process is the Appeals Council review. This part of the process is not always available, because the Appeals Council has the authority to decide whether or not to review any particular case. If the Council decides to review your case, it conducts a "paper" review of the entire file that has accumulated during the previous two steps. You have no opportunity to testify, although you may submit to the Council any additional documentation not submitted earlier.

Should I hire a lawyer if I want to appeal a decision of the Social Security Administration?

It is not strictly necessary to obtain a lawyer. But it is usually advisable to have some expert representation, since the appeal process is quite complicated and requires some understanding of the Social Security law and regulations. Legal Services attorneys are available for this purpose and can be contacted through your local Office for the Aging. Attorneys in private practice who specialize in law and aging are another important source for legal representation and advice. They may also be available to represent you at the various stages of the appeal process for a fee.

Is it useful to appeal Social Security decisions?

Yes. Since mistakes can quite easily be made by any large bureaucracy, including the Social Security Administration, it is often beneficial to appeal a decision that does not seem "right." Many controversies can be cleared up through the process. Furthermore, the Social Security Administration will not penalize you if you lose an appeal. Again, if in doubt, you should always request a reconsideration immediately, since there are time limits for filing the various appeals steps.

Where do I apply for a reconsideration or other administrative appeal?

A request for a reconsideration, an Administrative Law Judge hearing, or an Appeals Council review must be made at the local District Offices of the Social Security Administration. There are special forms available for this purpose.

Where can I get more information on the Social Security program?

A national toll-free telephone number (1-800-772-1213) is available on business days from 7 a.m. to 7 p.m. for information and assistance. When you call the Social Security Administration, you should have relevant Social Security numbers handy as well as any correspondence and forms. Another source for information is the local Social Security District Office, listed in the telephone directory.

CHAPTER

2

Supplemental Security Income

Financial Eligibility Tests . . . Other Eligibility Issues . . . Applying for Benefits . . . Changes in Benefits and Personal Circumstances . . . Appeals, Including Appeals of Overpayments.

Supplemental Security Income (SSI), administered by the Social Security Administration, is a federal program to meet the ordinary living expenses of people with incomes below the poverty level. SSI benefits are granted to three major categories of people (all of whom have to meet strict financial eligibility requirements): people age 65 and over; disabled people of any age; and the visually impaired of any age. In 1994, about 6.3 million people received SSI benefits.

SSI is a complicated program, governed by many rules and regulations that change often. That situation creates confusion for the program's beneficiaries as well as for the eligibility workers of the Social Security Administration. As in any large organization that administers a very complex program, mistakes are easily made. SSI applicants and recipients should always contact an impartial authority on SSI, such as a legal services attorney, if they have a question about information provided by the Social Security Administration. Furthermore, any time there is a question about a specific determination made by the Social Security Administration to deny, reduce, or terminate SSI benefits, an appeal should be filed with the local Social Security district office.

This chapter describes the eligibility requirements and benefits of the SSI program, how to apply, and how to appeal unfavorable decisions.

FINANCIAL ELIGIBILITY TESTS

Who is entitled to SSI benefits?

SSI is a program designed to meet the needs of people who have very low incomes and limited other financial resources; that is why it is sometimes called a "needs-based" program. In order to be eligible for SSI, applicants have to show that they have significant financial need. In contrast, Social Security benefits, which are based upon a person's prior work history, are available to anyone who has attained insured status, regardless of his or her financial situation.

Are SSI beneficiaries eligible for other public benefits?

Yes. In many states, SSI recipients are eligible for Medicaid, a needs-based health insurance program; for food stamps; and for state payment of the Medicare Part B premium. Check with your state office for the aging for other benefits for which you may be eligible. (See chapter 11 for resources to call.)

Can people receive both Social Security and SSI benefits?

Yes. If your income, counting your Social Security benefits and any other income you receive each month, is less than the SSI limit in your state (see next question) and you also have few other financial resources and you are 65, disabled, or visually impaired, you can receive SSI to supplement your other income up to the SSI limit.

What is the SSI income limit?

SSI income eligibility standards are different in different states, because some states have added a state supplement to the federal limit. In general, the federal income limit for a person living alone in 1995 was $478 per month. For a couple, the income limit was $707 per month in 1995. In states that offer a state supplement to SSI, the income limit is higher. To find out your state's SSI income limit, call 1-800-SSA-1213.

How much is the SSI benefit?

In 1995, if you had no other income, SSI would provide a federal maximum benefit of $458 per month (for individuals) and $687 per month (for couples). Some states provide additional state benefits, and in those states the maximum benefit levels would be higher. People don't usually obtain the maximum amount, however, because SSI is designed to "supplement" any other monthly income up to the maximum SSI level.

For example: Mr. Jones, a widower, has a combined income from Social Security and a small private pension of $300 per month. He lives in a state that does not provide for an additional state benefit. He will receive a federal SSI benefit of $178 each month. This figure is obtained by subtracting Mr. Jones' own income from the SSI income limit: $478 - $300 = $178. If Mr. Jones lived in a state that provides for a supplemental state benefit, both the income limit and the amount of the SSI benefit would be higher.

What is included in calculating "income"?

Apart from certain exempt items of income (discussed in the next question), the Social Security Administration counts both your unearned income and your earned income, and it counts "in-kind" income as well as money.

Unearned income is income that comes from Social Security, pensions, or interest on bank accounts.

Earned income is income obtained from work in the form of wages or tips. For example: Mrs. Dale earns about $100 a month by baby-sitting for her neighbor. This is considered earned income, and Mrs. Dale's SSI benefit will be affected by it. (Since SSI work rules are quite complex, it is wise to contact a legal services program in your area or your area agency on aging to obtain more detailed information on SSI earned income rules.)

In-kind income is any support you receive directly from another person which is not cash and which can be used to meet your need for food, clothing, or shelter — for example, free room and board or gifts of food or clothing. If each month, Mr. Adams receives from his best friend a bag of groceries with a value of $50, Mr. Adams has in-kind income of $50.

What kinds of income are exempt?

Income and earnings that are exempt from income considerations for SSI include:

- the first $20 of most income received in a month;
- the first $65 of earnings and one-half of earnings over $65 each month;
- the value of food stamps;
- income tax refunds;
- home energy assistance payments;
- small amounts of income received irregularly or infrequently;
- repayment of a loan you made to another person;
- payments from a trust for items other than food, clothing, or shelter (see question on trusts); and
- bill paid by someone else to cover your expenses for items other than food, clothing, or shelter (for example, telephone or medical bills).

What if I receive assistance from a community organization?

Assistance provided by community organizations that are incorporated as not-for-profit groups will not affect your SSI eligibility or benefits — as long as the organization meets the following conditions:

- it provides the help based on your individual need;
- it does not give you cash but provides you with food (such as a meal inside or outside your home), clothing, or rental payments made directly to your landlord; and

- it informs the Social Security Administration of such assistance to you.

What are the SSI limits on resources?

You are allowed to have up to $2,000 in savings and other resources if you are unmarried (couples can have up to $3,000). In addition, you are also allowed to have $1,500 set aside in a separate account for burial expenses (couples can set aside $3,000).

What exactly is meant by "resources"?

The Social Security Administration defines resources to include such items as:
- cash "on hand"
- bank accounts (checking and savings)
- stocks, bonds, mutual funds
- other personal property

This list is only partial and does not include everything counted as resources. Some specific kinds of property are discussed in the questions below.

Can I own a home or other property and still be eligible for SSI?

Yes, you are allowed to own certain items of value and still be eligible for SSI. Such property or resources include:
- the home you live in and the land it is on, regardless of its value;
- household goods and personal property that are not worth more than $2,000;
- one wedding ring and one engagement ring;

- one car, worth up to $4,500 (any additional value over $4,500 will be counted towards the $2,000 savings limit); or one car of any value, if the car is needed for employment, medical treatment, or performing essential daily activities;
- burial spaces for you and your immediate family (this includes a casket and burial container, plot, and headstone); and
- under certain circumstances, property held in a trust for you.

How is other real estate treated?

Any real estate you own, other than the home you live in, will be counted towards the $2,000 resource limit, unless one of the following conditions is met: (1) there is a legal impediment to selling the property; (2) the sale of the property would result in "undue hardship" to a joint owner because of loss of housing; or (3) a bona fide effort has been made to sell the property and it cannot be sold for any price.

Is a joint bank account counted towards the resource limit?

Yes, to the extent the money is yours, and perhaps even if it isn't yours. Joint bank accounts can pose special problems because when you apply for SSI the Social Security Administration will presume that all of the money held jointly by you and another person belongs to you (even when some of the money in the account belongs to the other account holder). You have to prove otherwise. So if you have a joint bank account with another person, it is important to save all deposit slips and statements so that you can present evidence to show that none or only some of the money belongs to you.

How are trusts treated for SSI purposes?

The answer to this question depends on the particular provisions of the trust instrument. Some trusts are not counted towards the SSI resource limit, others are. In order to ensure that the trust instrument will not disqualify you from SSI, certain conditions have to be met:

- you cannot have legal authority over how the trust funds are spent;
- an independent trustee has to manage the trust; and
- funds from the trust have to be paid directly to providers for services or items other than the beneficiary's food, clothing, or shelter.

Some trusts that are not counted as resources for SSI purposes may affect the Medicaid eligibility of the beneficiary. If you are considering setting up a trust, you should consult with a knowledgeable attorney.

Are life insurance policies considered when applying for SSI?

It depends. The Social Security Administration will count life insurance policies in different ways, depending on the type of policy you own.

Term life insurance policies, which by definition have no cash value, are not counted.

Life insurance policies with a face value of less than $1,500 are counted towards the $1,500 burial fund allowance. For policies with a face value of more than $1,500, the cash value is counted towards the $2,000 resource limit.

Can I dispose of my savings in order to become eligible for SSI?

Yes, currently you can dispose of your money in two ways.

You can give away money before applying for SSI and still be eligible for SSI benefits. The Social Security Administration will request that you show that the money is no longer in your possession and to whom the money was given.

You may also dispose of money by purchasing items for yourself. You will be expected to document what was purchased and what it cost. (You can purchase anything you wish, including luxury items.)

Keep in mind that transferring funds may affect your eligibility for Medicaid. Congress is considering legislation to change the SSI rules concerning transfers of assets. Before you transfer any money, you should consult a legal services or elder law attorney.

OTHER ELIGIBILITY ISSUES

Are there citizenship requirements to become eligible for SSI?

Yes. In order to qualify for SSI, you must be one of the following:

- a United States citizen;
- an alien lawfully admitted for permanent residence; or
- an alien permanently residing under "color of law" — that is, residing in the country with the knowledge

and permission of the Immigration and Naturalization Service.

Are there residency requirements to become eligible for SSI?

Yes, in order to be eligible for SSI you must live in the United States, including the District of Columbia and the Northern Mariana Islands; or be a child living with a parent in the military assigned to permanent duty overseas.

Residency in Puerto Rico, Guam, or the Virgin Islands does not count as residence in the United States.

If I live with another person, or in a group home, will my SSI be affected?

Yes, your living arrangement is one factor used to determine how much SSI you can receive. SSI benefits may vary depending upon where you live and who you live with.

If you live alone in your own place such as a house, apartment, or trailer, you may get up to the maximum SSI amount in your state.

If you live in someone else's household and pay your food and shelter costs, you may also qualify for the maximum SSI amount in your state. If you live in someone else's household and do not pay or pay only a part of your food and shelter costs, your SSI benefits may be reduced by up to one-third.

If you live in an adult home, family care home, or board home, you should contact your local Social Security Administration, because each state has its own laws concerning those facilities.

If you live in an institution such as a nursing home, you will be eligible for only up to $30 a month to pay for some personal items (some states offer additional amounts to nursing home residents).

How will a hospitalization affect my SSI benefits?

If you spend more than a full calendar month (defined as from the first of the month until the end of the month) in a hospital (or other facility) where Medicaid pays for more than half of the cost of your care, your SSI benefits will be reduced to about $30 a month during your hospital stay. Some states provide a supplement to this $30 payment.

How can I pay for my housing if I have only $30 a month?

If you expect to spend ninety days or less in a hospital, you can continue to receive your full SSI benefits for up to three months, if you provide certain documentation to the Social Security Administration. This information should include (1) a statement from a doctor that you will be in the facility for ninety days or less and (2) a statement from you that you need the SSI benefits to pay household expenses. Both statements have to be received by the ninetieth day of hospitalization or the day of discharge, whichever is earlier.

Can children be eligible for SSI?

Yes, disabled children can be eligible for SSI if they meet the disability standards (see chapter 3 on disability benefits). The Social Security Administration will count some of the parent's income and savings as available to the child and, after subtracting certain deductions, determine if the child is eligible for SSI.

Can a person whose spouse is not eligible for SSI be eligible?

Yes. However, the Social Security Administration will count some of the ineligible spouse's income and resources as available to the other spouse and determine if he or she is eligible for SSI.

APPLYING FOR BENEFITS

Where do I apply for SSI?

Applications for SSI can be made in person at the local district office of the Social Security Administration by filing a written application form or by telephone by calling the "teleservice centers" located around the country at 800-SSA-1213. If you do not file in person, you will be expected to send the completed application and the original supporting documents to the local district office. If you indicate an intent to file an application (by visiting or calling a Social Security office) you should receive a written notice informing you of the need to file an application within 60 days. If you are found eligible for SSI, you will be entitled to receive SSI benefits starting on the date you first indicated an intent to file for benefits.

What documents do I need to apply for SSI?

In order to establish your eligibility for SSI, you will need the following:

• Social Security card or number;

- Proof of age (birth certificate);
- Record of citizenship or alien status (passport or green card);
- Proof of income (copy of most recent social security or pension check or wage statements);
- Proof of resources (copies of bank books, stock certificates, bonds);
- Proof of living arrangements (copy of lease); and
- Medical records (if you are under 65 and applying for disability benefits).

If you cannot obtain the necessary documents, it is possible to provide substitute documents. In any case, never delay filing an application if you cannot assemble all of the needed documentation at once. File, and then consult with a knowledgeable attorney.

CHANGES IN BENEFITS AND PERSONAL CIRCUMSTANCES

Will my SSI benefit stay the same each year?

No. SSI recipients receive an increase in January of each year to reflect increases in the cost of living. Also, your SSI amount may change if your other income or your living arrangements change.

Once eligible for SSI, will I receive benefits forever?

Not necessarily, because the Social Security Administration will review your case from time to time and may decide to change your benefits. Some people have their cases reviewed each year while others have their cases reviewed less often. It all depends upon how frequently the

Social Security Administration expects your situation to change. At these so-called "recertifications," the Social Security Administration will ask you a series of questions concerning your income, savings, living arrangements, and medical condition (for those classified as disabled).

What changes in circumstances have to be reported to the Social Security Administration?

Some of the information which must be reported includes:

- change of address;
- change in living arrangement;
- change in income;
- change in savings;
- death of a spouse or anyone in the household;
- change in marital status;
- eligibility for other benefits;
- admission to or discharge from a hospital, nursing home, or other institution;
- for children, change in school attendance;
- improvement in medical condition of a disabled person; and
- leaving the United States.

This information should be reported as soon as possible but not later than ten days after the end of the month in which the event occurs.

What if I become unable to manage my own SSI income?

The Social Security Administration can appoint a representative payee — who can be a family member, friend, unrelated person, or nonprofit organization — to receive the SSI check and pay for a beneficiary's expenses. The representative payee is responsible for using the SSI benefit to pay for food, clothing, shelter, and medical expenses and has to save any benefits not needed for the beneficiary's immediate expenses. The representative payee must report to the Social Security Administration any changes in circumstances that may affect the recipient's eligibility for SSI. Finally, the representative payee has to submit annual reports to account for how the SSI benefits were spent. (See also chapter 1.)

Should the Social Security Administration be notified of the death of an SSI beneficiary?

Yes, the Social Security Administration has to be notified of the death of an SSI beneficiary. The SSI check that was received during the month a recipient dies and that has been cashed or deposited does not have to be returned. All other SSI checks of a deceased SSI beneficiary have to be returned. When the Social Security Administration owes SSI benefits to an SSI recipient (adult or child) who has died, the SSI benefits can be paid, under certain conditions, to a surviving spouse or parent.

APPEALS, INCLUDING APPEALS OF OVERPAYMENTS

What can I do if my application for SSI is denied?

You can file a written appeal to contest a Social Security Administration decision to deny your application. When in doubt, you should always file an appeal, since the Social Security Administration may be incorrect. There are many stages in the appeals process; if you lose at one stage, you may be able to win at the next. Chapter 1 has more details on how to appeal a decision before the Social Security Administration. Contact your local legal services office for assistance.

Can I appeal other Social Security Administration decisions about my SSI benefits?

Yes. Most decisions can be appealed, including determinations that your benefits are being reduced or stopped. Any time you wish to appeal a Social Security Administration decision, you should act immediately, since there are strict time limits for appealing most decisions.

One important group of appeals concerns "overpayments," discussed below.

What is meant by an "overpayment"?

The Social Security Administration defines an overpayment as SSI benefits you received when you were not eligible for them. When an overpayment has been made, the Social Security Administration will try to recover the money from you.

How can an overpayment occur?

SSI overpayments can be caused if you fail to report certain changes to the Social Security Administration and SSI benefits continue to be paid after the change. To avoid overpayments, you must report that:

• your income has changed;
• your savings have increased and exceeded the allowable limit;
• you were in a hospital;

- you left the country for more than thirty days;
- your living arrangements have changed; or
- your medical condition has improved and you are no longer disabled.

How can I appeal an SSI overpayment?

If you want to appeal an overpayment, you have two alternatives.

First, you can provide documentation that you were not overpaid. In order to show that the Social Security Administration has made a mistake, you will have to prove that you were eligible for SSI benefits during the contested time period and that the Social Security Administration is wrong in claiming that an event such as a change in your circumstances had occurred.

Or, instead of trying to prove you weren't overpaid, you can file a request for waiver of the overpayment. By seeking a waiver, you agree that the Social Security Administration is correct, but you request that you be found "without fault" in causing the overpayment. The Social Security Administration must then consider all factors that contributed to the overpayment, including any physical, mental, educational, or language limitations you have. Unlike most appeals, there is no deadline for filing a waiver.

What will happen if I lose the appeal?

The Social Security Administration will reduce your SSI check to recover the overpaid benefits. The check can be reduced by an amount equal to 10 percent of your total income. If you cannot live on such reduced benefits, you have the right to request that your SSI benefits be reduced by a smaller amount.

CHAPTER

3

Disability Benefits

*Eligibility . . . Determination of Disability . . .
Benefits . . . How to Apply . . . Appeals.*

The income benefits most Americans know as "disability benefits" are provided by two programs administered by the Social Security Administration: the Social Security disability program and the Supplemental Security Income (SSI) program. In 1994, an estimated 7 million Americans were receiving Social Security or SSI disability benefits.

The rules for establishing disability are the same for both programs. However, in order to be found eligible for disability benefits, applicants also have to establish general eligibility under the Social Security or SSI programs. Thus, in addition to being verifiably disabled, applicants for the Social Security disability program must establish that they have paid sufficiently into the Social Security system and have achieved "insured status for disability benefits" (see also chapter 1 on Social Security Old Age Benefits), while applicants for the SSI disability program must meet very strict income and resource limits (see also chapter 2 on Supplemental Security Income).

Since applicants have to submit extensive evidence of their disability to the Social Security Administration, the application process for disability benefits can be time-consuming and difficult. However, overcoming the bureaucratic hurdles through perseverance can result in receipt of vital benefits in the end. If an application for disability benefits is denied, the applicant has the right to appeal the determination; more than half of all appeals are successful.

This chapter focuses on how an applicant can establish medical and functional disability to meet the requirements of the Social Security and SSI disability programs.

ELIGIBILITY

Who can receive disability benefits?

The following people may be eligible for disability benefits:

- Disabled individuals who have attained "insured status for disability benefits" (for Social Security disability benefits)
- Disabled individuals who have low incomes and savings and who meet the income limits (for the Supplemental Security Income program)
- Disabled children
- Blind individuals
- Dependents or survivors of insured workers (see dependents and survivors benefits of the Social Security program in chapter 1)

How can I qualify for Social Security disability benefits?

To qualify for Social Security disability benefits, you must have worked long enough and recently enough under the Social Security system. You can earn up to a maximum of four quarters of coverage credits per year. The amount of earnings required for one quarter of coverage credit is $630 in 1995; this amount increases each year as general wage levels rise. See also chapter 1.

Note that family members who apply for benefits on the wage earner's work record do not themselves need work credits.

How many quarters of coverage are needed to qualify for Social Security disability benefits?

The number of work credits needed for Social Security disability benefits depends on the age you become disabled.

If you became disabled under age 24, you need six credits in the three-year period ending when the disability starts.

If you become disabled at age 24 to 30, you need credit for having worked half the time between 21 and the time you become disabled. For example, if you became disabled at age 27, you would need credit for three years of work (or one-half of six years).

If you became disabled at age 31 or older, the number of work credits you need is shown in table 3-1. Also, at least twenty of the credits (five years of work) must have been earned in the ten years immediately prior to your

TABLE 3-1
QUARTERS OF COVERAGE NEEDED
TO ACHIEVE INSURED STATUS FOR
SOCIAL SECURITY DISABILITY BENEFITS

Born after 1929 and disabled at age:	Credits needed
31 through 42	20
44	22
46	24
48	26
50	28
52	30
54	32
56	34
58	36
60	38
62 or older	40

becoming disabled. (This "recent work" rule does not apply to blind applicants, however.)

How do I qualify for Supplemental Security Income disability benefits?

To qualify for Supplemental Security Income disability benefits you don't have to have attained the "insured status for disability benefits" discussed above. However, you must meet the income and resource limits of the SSI program. Those limits are described in chapter 2, which explains how to obtain general SSI benefits.

How can blind persons receive disability benefits?

The Social Security Administration considers you blind if your vision cannot be corrected to better than 20/200 in the better eye, or if your visual field is 20 degrees or less even with a corrective lens. Both the Social Security and the SSI programs have special rules for persons who are blind. For example, the earnings limit for such a person is higher than the earnings limit that applies to nonblind disabled workers; and for blind SSI recipients, there are more generous rules regarding deductions for work expenses.

How can children obtain disability benefits?

Disabled children under age 18 (and students under 22) can receive disability benefits under the Supplemental Security Income program if they meet certain conditions. A child must have an impairment which (1) is identical or equivalent to one appearing on a specific list of qualifying impairments; or (2) significantly interferes with the child's ability to develop or function in an age-appropriate manner.

To learn how the child functions in various childhood activities, the Social Security Administration requires an "individualized functional assessment" which looks at the child's ability to function in such areas as understanding, communication, physical and social activities, and concentration. In addition to examining medical documentation of substantial mental or physical impairment, submitted by a doctor or licensed psychologist, the Social

Security Administration considers other information from people who have observed the child over a period of time (such as parents, social workers, child care providers, and school personnel).

There are special rules pertaining to eligibility for SSI disability benefits where the disability is due to HIV infection or to low birth weight. Check with your legal services organization or the local Social Security Administration office for more information.

Congress is considering legislation to change the SSI rules for disabled children. Consult with a legal services or elder law attorney for more information.

DETERMINATION OF DISABILITY

How does the Social Security Administration define disability?

You are considered disabled if you are "unable to engage in substantial gainful activity by reason of any medically determinable physical or mental impairment which can be expected to result in death or which has lasted or can be expected to last for a continuous period of not less than twelve months," taking into account your age, education, and past work history.

In simple terms, being disabled means that you are unable to work because of a medical condition that will last for at least one year.

What documentation do I need to establish that I am disabled?

The Social Security Administration requires medical documentation, including hospital admissions records, doctor or clinic notes, test results, and opinions of treating physicians and other health care providers. Most cases also require submission of vocational information, including a history of past work, and in some instances you will need proof of age, education, and training. Children who are applying for SSI disability benefits need to submit records from school, camp, day care, and similar sources in addition to medical evidence.

How is disability determined?

The Social Security Administration uses a process known as "sequential evaluation" to determine if you meet the definition for disability for both Social Security and SSI disability benefits. The disability determination focuses on five major questions:

(1) Are you performing so-called "substantial gainful activity"?
(2) Is your medical condition "severe"?
(3) Does your impairment meet or equal those of the "listing of impairments"?
(4) Can you, despite your condition, return to past "relevant" work?
(5) Can you perform any other work?

These questions are discussed more below.

Question one: are you performing "substantial gainful activity"?

"Substantial" work is work that involves significant physical or mental activity. It can include part-time work and work that pays less or involves less responsibility than your past employment.

"Gainful" work is work you do for pay or profit. It may also include work for which you receive no pay, as long as it is similar to work you once did for profit.

The Social Security Administration considers that any work averaging $500 per month or more is substantial gainful activity, while work that provides earnings averaging $300 or less is not substantial or gainful. Earnings falling between $300 and $500 will be evaluated together with other factors, such as whether the work performed was comparable to work performed by an unimpaired person and whether it was worth what the individual was paid.

If the Social Security Administration determines that you are performing substantial gainful activity, the application is denied no matter how disabled you might be. If it decides that you are not engaged in substantial gainful activity, the next step in the evaluation process begins.

Question two: is your medical condition "severe"?

The Social Security Administration next looks to see whether you have a severe impairment (or combination of impairments)—one that significantly limits your ability to do "basic work activities." Any limitation is enough if it significantly affects such basic work activities as:

- standing, walking, sitting, lifting, and carrying;
- seeing, hearing, and speaking;
- understanding and/or carrying out simple instructions;
- using judgment;
- responding appropriately to supervision and co-workers; and

• dealing with changes in a routine work setting.
Evidence of any appreciable limitation of function should establish the severity of your condition and lead to the next step.

Question three: does the impairment meet or equal a "listing"?

The "listing of impairments" is a part of federal regulations. It describes, for each major body part, those impairments that are considered severe enough to prevent a person from doing substantial gainful activity. You can automatically establish disability if your impairment is one of those listed. If your impairment (or combination of impairments) is different from those listed but is considered to be equally severe, you will be found to "equal" a listing. If your impairment meets or equals a listing, you will be found eligible; if not, the claim is evaluated under step four.

Question four: can you, despite your impairments, return to "past relevant work"?

The Social Security Administration considers "past relevant work" to be the work you performed within the past fifteen years. Whether you can perform past relevant work depends on your "residual functional capacity," that is, what you can still do despite your limitations. If the Social Security Administration determines that you can perform past relevant work, benefits will be denied. If it determines that you cannot, the claim goes to the last step.

Question five: can you perform any other work?

In the final step, the Social Security Administration determines whether you can perform work other than the work you used to do. Your age, education, and work history are considered. You may be determined not disabled if you have the residual functional capacity to perform other work which exists in significant numbers in the national economy (even if you cannot find a job). Generally, the older you are, the less education you have, the less skilled your past work, and the more limited you are in physical activities, the more likely you will be determined disabled. The Social Security Administration must also take into account problems you may have with nonphysical activities, such as remembering, following instructions, paying attention, concentrating, or even travelling.

BENEFITS

How much can I receive in disability benefits?

The amount you receive depends on the type of benefit you receive.

If you receive Social Security disability benefits, the amount depends on your work history and how much you have paid into the Social Security system (see chapter 1 for more details).

If you receive Supplemental Security Income benefits, the amount depends on other income you may have (see chapter 2 for more details).

Once established, do Social Security disability benefits continue forever?

It depends. From time to time, the Social Security Administration will reevaluate your disability to determine if you are still disabled or blind. This reevaluation is called a "continuing disability review." How often your case is reviewed depends on the type of disability you have.

If the Social Security Administration determines that you are no longer disabled or blind, it will stop your benefits. That decision can be appealed.

Is this review the same for Supplemental Security Income disability benefits?

If you receive Supplemental Security Income disability benefits, you are subject to the continuing disability review mentioned above. If you are determined to be no longer disabled, your disability benefits will end. But your income and resources are also subject to review. If your income and/or resources are more than the allowable limits, you may be terminated from the Supplemental Security Income program, even if you are still disabled. If your income and resources have been over the allowable limit for a period of time, you can be charged with a so-called "overpayment." As with all Social Security Administration determinations, such terminations and overpayments can be appealed.

Are there special rules about the effect of work on disability benefits?

Yes. If you are a recipient of Social Security disability benefits, you are allowed to return to work without losing any benefits, provided you continue to meet the definition of disability. For a period of nine months, called a "trial work period," there is no limit on how much you can earn. If, after the ninth month, you continue to earn an average of $500 or more per month, Social Security disability benefits will be terminated. In determining your earnings, the Social Security Administration will exempt certain disability-related work expenses.

The work rules for Supplemental Security Income disability benefits are different. Disabled and blind SSI recipients who continue to meet the definition of disability can return to work for as long as they want. However, their SSI benefits will be reduced as a result of their wages. Again, the Social Security Administration exempts the costs of certain disability-related items and services the worker needs in order to be employed (for example, the cost of car modifications or attendant care).

A disabled or blind individual who is receiving Social Security and/or Supplemental Security Income disability benefits may also set up a special savings plan to put aside funds to meet expenses related to reaching an occupational goal in the future. The Social Security Administration will not count income or resources set aside under this Plan for Achieving Self-Support (PASS plan) and will not reduce SSI benefits if the plan is in writing and approved by the Social Security Administration.

If the disabled worker dies, will Social Security disability benefits be discontinued for his or her survivors?

Not necessarily. Certain family members may continue to qualify for Social Security disability benefits on the deceased wage-earner's record if they meet certain conditions. Those who may be entitled include the following:

- Disabled widows or widowers who are at least 50 but under 59 years of age, if the disability began before the spouse's death or within seven years after the spouse's death. (If the widow or widower is caring for children and receiving Social Security benefits, she or he is eligible if the disability begins before those payments end or within seven years after they end.)
- Nondisabled widows (or widowers) age 60 or older who are not working.
- Disabled ex-wives or ex-husbands age 50 or older, if the marriage lasted at least ten years.

Nondisabled surviving spouses can qualify for old age nondisability benefits at age 60.

HOW TO APPLY

Where can I apply for disability benefits?

You can apply for disability benefits under both the Social Security and SSI programs at a local Social Security office. For the location of the nearest district office, check your local telephone directory or call 1-800-SSA-1213.

How long does it take for Social Security to act on my application?

There is no specific time by which the Social Security Administration must make a decision. The amount of time depends on the complexities of each case and available staff at the Social Security Administration office who review the applications; decisions can take up to twelve months or longer.

Once I have established eligibility for disability benefits, how long will it take to receive them?

For those who applied for Social Security disability benefits and who have been successful in establishing their eligibility, there is a five-month waiting period before disability payments begin. However, benefits will be paid retroactively up to twelve months prior to the application date (if you were disabled during that period).

For SSI disability, there is no waiting period, but benefits cannot be paid prior to the application date.

APPEALS

What can I do if I have been found ineligible for disability benefits?

The sequential evaluation process is obviously very complicated, and it is always possible that you will be found not disabled enough to meet the strict eligibility criteria of the Social Security Administration. It is particularly important in the context of disability determinations to appeal any decision that denies you benefits. If your application is denied, you should contact an attorney who is an expert in disability benefits and file an appeal with the Social Security Administration. The appeals process for disability determinations is similar to that outlined in chapter 1.

CHAPTER

4

Veterans' Benefits

General Eligibility Requirements ... Compensation for Service-Connected Disability ... Pensions for Disabled Veterans ... Financial Benefits for Dependents of Veterans ... Financial Benefits for Survivors of Veterans ... Health Care Benefits ... Burial Benefits ... How to Apply ... Appeals.

The United States Department of Veterans Affairs (VA) offers numerous benefits to America's veterans, their dependents, and their survivors. Veterans' benefits include income benefits, health care benefits, burial benefits, life insurance, home loan guarantees, education and training, and employment assistance. The VA operates 158 medical centers, consisting of 171 hospitals and more than 200 outpatient clinics. In 1991, about 2.2 million veterans made more than 20 million outpatient visits to these centers and had more than 970,000 hospital stays. Of these veterans, about 1 million had disabilities incurred during military service and 1.2 million had disabilities unrelated to military service.

Almost 3 million veterans receive disability compensation or pension benefits, and another 1 million spouses and other dependents receive additional compensation.

59

The number of veterans over the age of 65 is increasing dramatically. In 1980, about 25 percent of all American men age 65 and older were veterans; by the year 2000, an expected 60 percent of all elderly men will be veterans and eligible for some veterans' benefits. They will need information about a large bureaucratic system that provides income assistance and health care services in addition to an array of other supportive services.

This chapter focuses on the disability, pension, health care, and burial benefits available to veterans, their spouses, children, dependent parents, and survivors. It also provides an overview of the major administrative and appeals procedures of the VA.

GENERAL ELIGIBILITY REQUIREMENTS

Are all veterans eligible for veterans' benefits?

Generally, eligibility for most veterans' benefits is based on discharge from "active" military service under "other than dishonorable" conditions.

What is "active" service?

Active service means full-time service for a specific period of time, as a member of the Army, Navy, Air Force, Marines, or Coast Guard or as a commissioned officer of the Public Health Service, the Environmental Services Administration, or the National Oceanic and Atmospheric Administration.

In addition, wartime service in twenty-six organizations (listed in the appendix at the end of this chapter) has been certified as active military service.

What is considered "other than dishonorable" discharge?

Honorable and general discharges are discharges considered "other than dishonorable" and qualify the veteran for VA benefits.

Are any other types of discharges a bar to veterans' benefits?

Yes, in addition to dishonorable discharges, two other types of discharges — undesirable discharges and bad conduct discharges — may disqualify you from obtaining veterans' benefits depending on the circumstances.

Are all veterans entitled to the same benefits?

No. Once a veteran has met the general eligibility requirements, other factors are considered to determine the specific benefit the veteran will be entitled to. These factors may include:

- the veteran's service history
- the veteran's discharge status
- whether the veteran is disabled, and whether the disability is service-connected or non-service-connected
- the veteran's income
- the size of the veteran's household

Who can qualify for veterans' benefits?

Veterans' benefits are available to:

- veterans with a service-connected disability;
- low income veterans with a non-service-connected disability;
- the spouses of veterans;
- the dependent children of veterans;

- the dependent parents of veterans; and
- the survivors of veterans.

What benefits are available to veterans and their families?

Federal veterans' benefits include financial benefits (see next question); medical benefits in the form of hospital care, nursing home care, and outpatient care; and other services, including burial benefits, education and training, vocational rehabilitation, life insurance, and home loan guaranties. This is a partial list of federal benefits.

In some areas, there are also state and local government benefits earmarked for veterans and their families. Check with your state and local governments to find out if they offer programs specifically for veterans.

What types of financial compensation are available to veterans and their families?

- Service-connected disability compensation;
- Non-service-connected pension benefits (for low-income veterans);
- Dependency and indemnity compensation; and
- Death compensation.

COMPENSATION FOR SERVICE-CONNECTED DISABILITY

How do I qualify for service-connected disability compensation?

Veterans who were disabled by injury or disease that was incurred or aggravated during active military service may be eligible for disability compensation. The amount you will receive depends on your personal circumstances and is decided on an individual basis. Disability compensation is determined on the basis of the effects of the injury or disease; the disability is measured in increments of 10 percent. The monthly payments effective for 1995 are set forth in table 4-1.

Furthermore, when you are adjudged to have suffered certain specific, severe disabilities, additional funds may be available.

TABLE 4-1
DEGREE OF DISABILITY
AND COMPENSATION RATES, 1995

Disability	Monthly rate
10 percent	$ 89
20	170
30	260
40	371
50	529
60	666
70	841
80	974
90	1,096
100	1,823

PENSIONS FOR DISABLED VETERANS

How can I qualify for a non-service-connected pension?

You can receive a pension if you are a low-income disabled veteran. You must meet three basic tests:

- You are totally (100 percent) and permanently disabled from a cause not related to your military service.
- Your income and resources are below certain limits.
- You have at least ninety days of military service, at least one day of which was during a period of war (you need not have been in combat).

Pension benefits are affected by the size of the veteran's household, and benefits are reduced by a veteran's "countable income." Countable income is the amount of income considered after deducting certain items, such as unreimbursed medical expenses. Surviving widows of wartime veterans may be eligible for these benefits if they meet the income and resource requirements.

Additional income benefits also may be available for veterans receiving pensions who are permanently "housebound" or in need of the "aid and attendance" of another person.

What is meant by "housebound"?

You are considered housebound by the VA when you are rated 100 percent for a single permanent disability and also meet any one of the following tests:

- You have additional disabilities rated at 60 percent or more.

- You are substantially confined to the home.
- You are institutionalized because of the disability and the confinement is likely to continue for life.

Housebound benefits are paid to a veteran or surviving spouse.

How can I establish that I need the "aid and attendance" of another person?

Your need for aid and attendance can be established when you fit into one of the following categories:
- You are in a nursing home.
- You are blind or visually impaired.
- You are bedridden.
- You require assistance in activities such as dressing, bathing, or feeding.

Aid and attendance benefits are payable to a veteran or surviving spouse.

Once I have been found eligible for a VA pension, will I always receive the same amount?

Not necessarily. For instance, when a veteran who has no spouse, child, or dependent parent is institutionalized (which includes hospitalization, nursing home care, and domiciliary care) and the VA is paying for care, the pension is reduced to $90 per month after three full calendar months of care. However, if nursing home care is continued for the primary purpose of providing the veteran with rehabilitation services, the pension is not reduced.

How is the amount of pension benefits computed?

The method of computing veterans' pension benefits has been revised several times.

The VA Improved Pension Program covers veterans who applied for benefits after December 31, 1978 (for veterans who applied for benefits before that date, other methods are used to determine pension benefits). The payment is reduced by the amount of countable income of the veteran and any spouse or dependent children. See table 4-2.

Are there resource limits that apply to the improved pension program?

There is no specific resource amount that makes someone ineligible for benefits. The VA examines the market value of all real and personal property owned by the veteran and determines if it should be used for the veteran's maintenance. In making the determination, the VA considers many factors, including the veteran's life expectancy, the number of dependents, and the potential rate of depletion of the veteran's estate.

Which resources are not considered?

The VA does not consider the value of the family home, automobile, or any property that cannot readily be converted to cash.

Can veterans transfer or give away their resources and become eligible for pension benefits?

It depends. If resources are transferred to a relative living in the household of the veteran, there is a presumption that the value of the veteran's estate has not been reduced. However, if property is transferred to someone outside of the household, the value of the veteran's estate

TABLE 4-2
VETERANS' BENEFITS UNDER
IMPROVED PENSION PROGRAM, 1995

Recipient	Monthly benefit
Veteran without dependent spouse or child	$ 670
Veteran with one dependent spouse or child	877
Veteran in need of regular aid and attendance with no dependents	1,071
Veteran in need of regular aid and attendance with one dependent	1,279
Veteran permanently housebound with no dependents	819
Veteran permanently housebound with one dependent	1,026
Two veterans married to each other	877
Increase for each additional dependent child	114

is reduced if the veteran relinquishes all rights of owner-ship.

Since the transfer of resources may affect eligibility for other public benefits, veterans should consult with an attorney knowledgeable about veterans' law and other public entitlement programs such as Medicaid.

FINANCIAL BENEFITS FOR DEPENDENTS OF VETERANS

Can the dependents of veterans with service-connected disabilities receive additional payments?

Yes, the dependents of veterans with service-connected disabilities can get payments, depending upon the veteran's level of disability. Veterans whose service-connected disabilities are rated at 30 percent or more are entitled to additional monthly compensation for dependents. The additional amount is determined according to the number of dependents and the degree of disability. In addition, the spouse of a disabled veteran rated 30 percent or more is also entitled to receive a special allowance if the spouse needs the aid and attendance of another person.

FINANCIAL BENEFITS FOR SURVIVORS OF VETERANS

What benefits are available to survivors of veterans whose death was due to a service-connected disability?

Dependency and Indemnity Compensation (DIC) payments may be made on the record of a deceased veteran whose death was caused by a service-connected disability due to (1) a disease or injury incurred or aggravated in the line of duty or (2) a disability for which the VA is paying benefits (the veteran's death cannot be the result of willful misconduct). Payments may be made to the following survivors:

- spouses
- unmarried children under 18
- certain children who, prior to reaching age 18, became permanently incapable of self-support
- children between 18 and 23 if attending a VA-approved school
- low-income parents.

What benefits are available to survivors of veterans whose death was not due to a service-connected cause?

Dependency and indemnity compensation payments may be authorized on the record of a veteran who had a total service-connected disability at the time of death, but whose death was not the result of their service-connected disability, if the veteran was either (1) continuously rated totally disabled for ten or more years up until death, or (2) so rated for at least five years from the date of discharge from military service.

Dependency and indemnity compensation is available to surviving spouses; unmarried children under age 18; certain children who, prior to reaching age 18, became permanently incapable of self-support; and children between ages 18 and 23 if attending a VA-approved school.

How much dependency and indemnity compensation do surviving spouses receive?

The amount of DIC paid to a surviving spouse depends on the date of death of the veteran.

If the veteran died on or after January 1, 1993, the surviving spouse receives $790 a month. An additional $173 a month will be paid if the deceased veteran had been entitled to receive 100 percent service-connected compensation for at least eight years immediately preceding death and the surviving spouse was married to the veteran for those same eight years.

If the veteran died before January 1, 1993, the amount paid to the surviving spouse is based upon the veteran's pay grade and varies from $790 to $1,681 a month. Surviving spouses who remarry will have their payments terminated.

Are there other special payments available to surviving spouses and parents?

Yes. Surviving spouses and parents receiving dependency and indemnity compensation may be granted a special allowance if they are patients in a nursing home, or require the aid and attendance of another person, or are permanently housebound. The additional allowance for a surviving spouse who needs aid and attendance or is a patient in a nursing home is $200 monthly. Surviving spouses receiving DIC who are not so disabled as to require the regular aid and attendance of another person, but who are permanently housebound, may be granted an additional allowance of $97.

What benefits are available to survivors of veterans who were not totally disabled and who died from non-service-connected causes?

Low-income surviving spouses, unmarried children under age 18, or unmarried children until age 23 (if attending a VA-approved school) may be eligible for a needs-based non-service-connected pension if the deceased veteran met the following conditions:

- The veteran was not dishonorably discharged.
- The veteran either (1) had at least ninety days of active military service, at least one day of which was during a period of war, or (2) had a service-connected disability.

Pensions are not payable to those with estates large enough to provide maintenance. A surviving spouse who is a patient in a nursing home, in need of aid and attendance, or permanently housebound may be entitled to higher income limitations or additional benefits. Children who became permanently incapable of self-support because of a disability before reaching age 18 may be eligible for a pension as long as the condition exists, unless the child's income exceeds the applicable limit or the child marries.

What are the payments under the non-service-connected death pension program?

The Improved Pension Program provides a monthly supplement to other income, such as Social Security benefits, to bring your total countable income up to an established level. See table 4-3. Countable income may be reduced by medical expenses.

TABLE 4-3
SURVIVORS' BENEFITS UNDER
IMPROVED PENSION PROGRAM, 1995

Recipient	Monthly benefit
Surviving spouse with no dependent children	$ 449
Surviving spouse with one dependent child	588
Surviving spouse in need of regular aid and attendance with no dependent children	718
Surviving spouse in need of regular aid and attendance with one dependent child	857
Surviving spouse permanently housebound with no dependent children	549
Surviving spouse permanently housebound with one dependent child	688
Increase for each additional dependent child	114
Pension rates for each surviving child	114

HEALTH CARE BENEFITS

What services are covered by the health care program of the VA?

The VA provides for a wide array of medical services, including:
- hospital care
- nursing home care
- domiciliary care (rehabilitative and long-term care for veterans who require minimal medical care but who

do not need the skilled nursing services provided in nursing homes)

- outpatient medical treatment and services (including examinations, prosthetic devices, dental care, alcohol and drug dependence treatment, medications, rehabilitation, mental health services, and home health services)

What are the eligibility requirements for hospital and nursing home care?

Eligibility depends upon the category—"mandatory" or "discretionary"—in which a veteran is included. The mandatory category includes veterans who

- have service-connected disabilities;
- were exposed to herbicides while serving in Vietnam;
- were exposed to ionizing radiation in the occupation of Hiroshima and Nagasaki;
- have a condition related to service in the Persian Gulf;
- are former prisoners of war;
- are receiving a VA pension;
- are veterans of the Mexican Border period or World War I; or
- are eligible for Medicaid; or
- have non-service-connected disabilities and income of $20,469 or less if single with no dependents, or $24,565 or less if married or single with one dependent (the income limit is raised $1,368 for each additional dependent).

The VA *must* provide hospital care and *may* provide nursing care to veterans in the mandatory category if space and resources are available.

The discretionary category includes veterans who have a non-service-connected condition and income higher than $20,469 if single with no dependents, or higher than $24,565 if married or single with one dependent. For these veterans, the VA *may* provide hospital and nursing home care if space and resources are available in VA facilities.

Does the VA charge veterans for hospital care?

There is no charge for veterans who fall into the mandatory category. Veterans in the discretionary category are charged up to the cost of hospital care or an amount equal to the Medicare deductible ($716 in 1995), whichever is less, for the first ninety days of hospital care in a 365 day period and up to $358 for each additional ninety-day period. In addition, there is a charge of $10 per day for hospital care.

Does the VA charge veterans for nursing home care?

There is no charge for veterans in the mandatory category. Veterans in the discretionary category are charged up to the cost of nursing home care or an amount equal to the Medicare deductible ($716 in 1995), whichever is less, for each ninety days of nursing home care received in a year. In addition, there is a charge of $5 per day for nursing home stays.

Are there other limits on nursing home care?

Yes. The VA will provide nursing home coverage to veterans who require nursing home care for a service-connected disability and veterans who had been discharged from a VA medical center and are receiving home health

services from a VA medical center. The VA usually autho-
rizes care for up to six months but can provide additional
coverage for veterans who require nursing home care due
to a service-connected disability or for veterans who
were hospitalized primarily for treatment of a service-
connected disability. Nursing home care may be approved for non-service-connected veterans whose income exceeds the above income limits if space is available.

What are the eligibility criteria for receiving outpatient medical treatment?

The VA *must* furnish outpatient care without limitation
to veterans in the following categories:
- all veterans, for service-connected disabilities;
- veterans with a 50 percent or more service-connected
  disability, for any disability; and
- veterans who have suffered an injury as a result of VA
  hospitalization for that condition only.

In addition, the VA *must* furnish outpatient care for any
condition to prevent the need for hospitalization, to prepare for hospitalization, or to complete treatment after
hospital care, nursing home care, or domiciliary care to
veterans in two other categories:
- veterans whose service-connected disabilities are
  rated between 30 and 40 percent; and
- veterans whose annual income is not greater than the
  pension rate of veterans in need of regular aid and attendance (discussed earlier in this chapter).

The VA also *may* provide outpatient care to other veterans.

Is medical coverage available for dependents and survivors of veterans?

Yes. The Civilian Health and Medical Program of the Veterans Administration (CHAMPVA) provides medical coverage for:

- the spouse or child of a veteran who has a permanent and total service-connected disability;
- the surviving spouse or child of a veteran who died as a result of a service-connected condition or who at the time of death was permanently and totally disabled from a service-connected condition; and
- the surviving spouse or child of a person who died while on active military service.

BURIAL BENEFITS

What burial benefits does the VA provide?

Members of the armed forces who die on active duty and veterans who are discharged or separated from active duty under conditions other than dishonorable are eligible for the following benefits:

- burial in a VA national cemetery;
- burial of spouses and minor children of eligible veterans in a VA national cemetery;
- a burial allowance of up to $1,500 if the veteran's death is service-connected;
- a $300 burial and funeral expense allowance for a veteran who died from a non-service-connected disability (if the veteran was entitled to receive pension or compensation benefits) or who died while in a VA fa-

cility or nursing home with which the VA contracted; and

- a headstone or marker for the veteran's burial.

HOW TO APPLY

How do I apply for veterans' benefits?

The Department of Veterans Affairs (VA), through its regional offices, processes claims for veterans' benefits. Call 1-800-827-1000 for the regional office in your area. Many state governments and some municipalities operate agencies which assist veterans in filing claims and administer state and local veterans' programs. Many veterans' service organizations also provide information and assistance.

What documentation is needed to file a claim?

In order to file any claim with the VA (or to obtain information or assistance), the identity of the veteran is vitally important. The following documentation is sufficient to establish the veteran's identity:

- the veteran's file number (if the veteran had filed a prior claim); or
- a copy of the veteran's service discharge form; or
- the veteran's full name, Social Security number, military service number, branch of service, and dates of service.

Once a claim is filed, the veteran's VA file number or Social Security number identifies the veteran.

What documentation is needed to file for veterans' death benefits?

In order to file for death benefits, the claimant must document the fact that the veteran has died and must also establish the claimant's own identity and relationship with the veteran. The following documentation is needed:

- the veteran's death certificate (if the veteran died in a hospital not administered by the VA);
- the veteran's marriage certificate for spouse's or children's benefits;
- the child's birth certificate for children's benefits;
- the veteran's birth certificate (for parents who wish to establish eligibility).

APPEALS

Can I appeal a decision made by the VA?

Yes, veterans (and their dependents or survivors) have the right to appeal determinations made by the VA. Typical issues that can be appealed are the amount of compensation or pension benefits, eligibility for medical benefits, and waivers of alleged overpayments. How do I appeal a decision?

A claimant has to file an appeal within one year of the date on the initial determination. There are several steps in the VA's appeals process.

Step One: The appeals process starts by filing a "notice of disagreement" with the VA agency or facility responsible for making the initial determination. Once the notice of disagreement has been filed, the claimant will receive a "statement of the case," explaining how the agency or facility had arrived at the initial determination. If the claimant still feels that the VA has made a mistake, the claimant can go to step two.

Step Two: What is called a "substantive appeal" has to be filed with the Board of Veterans' Appeals within sixty days of the date on the statement of the case, or within one year of the date of the initial determination. When the Board decides the case, it sends a "notice of decision" to the claimant. If the decision after appeal is negative, the claimant can go to step three.

Step Three: This step takes the case to a specialized court. A "notice of appeal" has to be filed with the Court of Veterans Appeals within 120 days of the date the notice of decision was mailed by the Board of Veterans' Appeals. The jurisdiction of the Court of Veterans Appeals is limited: it has the power to consider only cases in which a notice of disagreement was filed on or after November 18, 1988 (the date when the court came into being). For information on the court's rules and procedures, call 1-800-869-8654.

Step Four: Decisions of the Court of Veterans Appeals may be appealed to the U.S. Court of Appeals for the Federal Circuit and from there to the Supreme Court of the United States.

Prior to filing a substantive appeal with the Board of Veterans' Appeals, an individual can also request a "hearing" before the agency which made the original determination. The time limits for filing a notice of disagreement or a substantive appeal must be adhered to despite the request for a hearing.

Appendix

Special Groups Eligible for Veterans' Benefits

A number of groups who have provided military-related service to the United States have been granted VA benefits. For the service to qualify, the Defense Secretary must certify that the group has provided active military service. Individual members must be issued a discharge by the Defense Secretary to qualify for VA benefits.

Service in the following groups has been certified as active military service for benefits purposes:

1. Women's Air Forces Services Pilots (WASPs).
2. Signal Corps Female Telephone Operators Unit of World War I.
3. Engineer Field Clerks.
4. Women's Army Auxiliary Corps (SAAC).
5. Quartermaster Corps female clerical employees serving with the AEF (American Expeditionary Forces) in World War I.
6. Civilian employees of Pacific Naval Air Bases who actively participated in defense of Wake Island during World War II.
7. Reconstruction aides and dietitians in World War I.
8. Male civilian ferry pilots.
9. Wake Island Defenders from Guam.

10. Civilian personnel assigned to the secret intelligence element of the OSS.
11. Guam Combat Patrol.
12. Quartermaster Corps Keswick crew on Corregidor (WWII).
13. United States civilian volunteers who actively participated in the defense of Bataan.
14. United States merchant seamen who served on blockships in support of Operation Mulberry.
15. American merchant marines in oceangoing service during the period of armed conflict, Dec. 7, 1941, to Aug. 15, 1945.
16. Civilian Navy IFF technicians who served in the combat areas of the Pacific during World War II, Dec. 7, 1941, to Aug. 15, 1945.
17. United States civilians of the American Field Service who served overseas in World War I between Aug. 31, 1917, and Jan. 1, 1918.
18. United States civilians of the American Field Service who served overseas under U.S. armies and U.S. army groups in World War II between Dec. 7, 1941, and May 8, 1945.
19. United States civilian employees of American Airlines who served overseas in a contract with the Air Transport Command between Dec. 14, 1941, and Aug. 14, 1945.
20. Civilian crewmen of U.S. Coast and Geodetic Survey vessels who served in areas of immediate military hazard while conducting cooperative operations with and for the U.S. Armed Forces between Dec. 7, 1941, and Aug. 15, 1945.

21. Honorably discharged members of the American Volunteer Group (Flying Tigers) who served between Dec. 7, 1941, and July 18, 1942.
22. United States civilian flight crew and aviation ground support employees of United Air Lines who served overseas in a contract with Air Transport Command between Dec. 14, 1941, and Aug. 14, 1945.
23. United States civilian flight crew and aviation ground support employees of Transcontinental and Western Air Inc. (TWA), who served overseas in a contract with the Air Transport Command between Dec. 14, 1941, and Aug. 14, 1945.
24. United States civilian flight crew and aviation ground support employees of Consolidated Vultee Aircraft Corp. (Consairway Division) who served overseas in a contract with Air Transport Command between Dec. 14, 1941, and Aug. 14, 1945.
25. U.S. civilian flight crew and aviation ground support employees of Pan American World Airways and its subsidiaries and affiliates, who served overseas in a contract with the Air Transport Command and Naval Air Transport Service between Dec. 14, 1941, and Aug. 14, 1945.
26. Honorably discharged members of the American Volunteer Guard, Eritrea Service Command, between June 21, 1942, and March 31, 1943.

Except where specific dates are mentioned in the list above, a member of one of these groups must have served during one of the following wartime periods:

- Persian Gulf War: August 2, 1990, through a date to be set
- Vietnam Era: August 5, 1964, through May 7, 1975
- Korean Conflict: June 27, 1950, through January 31, 1955
- World War II: December 7, 1941, through December 31, 1946
- World War I: April 6, 1917, through November 11, 1918 (for W.W. I veterans who served in Russia, extended to April 1, 1920; and for those who had at least one day of service between April 6, 1917, and November 11, 1918, extended to July 1, 1921)
- Mexican Border Period: May 9, 1916, through April 5, 1917 (for veterans who served in Mexico, on its borders, or in adjacent waters).

CHAPTER

5

Medicare

General Eligibility Requirements . . . Enrollment . . .
Medicare Benefits . . . Appeals . . . Auxiliary Medicare
Benefits.

Medicare, the nation's most important health insurance
program for the elderly, was initiated in 1965 to address the
medical needs of Americans age 65 and over. In 1972, coverage was extended to include disabled persons under age
65. By 1994, an estimated 37 million elderly and disabled
were entitled to Medicare, including 32.8 million persons
65 and over and 4.2 million disabled people under the age
of 65.

Medicare has two parts, Part A and Part B. They provide
for different types of coverage. Part A covers acute care in
hospitals, limited skilled nursing home care, and limited
skilled home care and hospice care. Part B covers physician
services, medical tests, outpatient services, and durable
medical equipment. Although Medicare is a major health
care benefit program, it has some serious shortcomings and
does not cover all of the care people need as they age.

Eligibility for parts A and B is established in two different ways. Everyone who is eligible for Social Security old age benefits is automatically eligible for Part A. Part B, on the other hand, is an optional service that requires the payment of a premium.

Financing of Medicare is also different for parts A and B. Medicare Part A is financed by employees and employers who make contributions to the Social Security system; Part B is financed in part by general tax revenues (75 percent) and in part by the premiums charged to beneficiaries (25 percent).

While the federal government (through the Health Care Financing Administration of the United States Department of Health and Human Services) oversees the Medicare program and sets policy and guidelines, the daily administrative duties are handled by private insurance companies who process claims for Medicare payment. Insurance companies have been known to interpret guidelines from the federal government overly restrictively; as a result, claims are incorrectly denied or are inadequately reimbursed. Like all other public entitlement programs, the Medicare program provides for the opportunity to appeal decisions that were made by the insurance companies or the providers. Medicare beneficiaries should, therefore, be prepared to file appeals if they believe that their claims have not been adequately covered.

This chapter describes the eligibility requirements of Parts A and B, enrollment, the benefits of both parts, and administrative and appeals procedures.

GENERAL ELIGIBILITY REQUIREMENTS

How do I know if I am eligible for Medicare?

You are eligible for Medicare if you:

- are entitled to Social Security old age benefits and are age 65 or older; or
- have been entitled to Social Security disability benefits for twenty-four months; or
- are suffering from end-stage renal disease.

Can I obtain Medicare at age 62 if I start receiving Social Security benefits then?

No. You are not eligible for Medicare until you are 65. As noted in chapter 1, you can start receiving reduced Social Security benefits as early as age 62. But even if you do, you will have to wait until you are 65 for Medicare. The only people under age 65 who can obtain Medicare are those who have been collecting Social Security disability benefits for twenty-four months or more and those who suffer from end-stage renal disease.

Are there any financial tests for Medicare?

No. Medicare eligibility is not based upon how much income and savings you have. Instead, it is based upon your eligibility to receive Social Security benefits, regardless of your financial situation. Medicare is therefore not a needs-based program, but is more like an insurance program.

Can I have both Medicare and health insurance through my employer after I reach age 65?

Yes. If you work for an employer with at least twenty employees (or if you are covered under a spouse's health plan), you are allowed to choose whether Medicare or the work plan will be the "primary" payor.

If you select the work plan as the primary payor, you have the option of enrolling in Medicare. If you enroll in Medicare, Medicare is the secondary payor and may pay benefits (known as secondary benefits) depending upon the service, the amount paid by the work plan, and Medicare's coverage rules.

If you select Medicare as the primary payor, then your employer plan is allowed to pay only for services not covered by Medicare (for example, dental work and hearing aids). The employer plan is not allowed to pay the "deductibles" and "co-payments" not covered by Medicare.

Are there any other situations where Medicare might be the secondary payor?

Yes. Medicare is also required to be the secondary payor in cases of (1) workers' compensation coverage and (2) automobile, no-fault, or liability insurance coverage. In other words, the workers' compensation plan, no-fault, or liability insurer must be billed first, before any attempts are made to collect from Medicare. Although Medicare benefits are secondary, Medicare may pay first if those other insurers will not pay within 120 days. In such cases, however, Medicare will recover the payments when the other insurer pays.

Can I have both Medicare and Medicaid?

Yes, if you meet the income and resource requirements for Medicaid and you are 65 years old or have been disabled for twenty-four months, you can be eligible for both Medicare and Medicaid (for Medicaid eligibility requirements, see chapter 6).

If I select my employer's plan as the primary payor, can I enroll any time I want for Medicare?

If you are over 65 and covered by an employer group health plan, you can enroll during a "special enrollment period" and not face a penalty on your Part B premium. The special enrollment period starts the month you are no longer working or are no longer covered by the employer plan, whichever comes first, and it ends seven months later. You should enroll during the first month of the special enrollment period so that your Part B coverage will start immediately.

Do I have to pay for Medicare coverage?

It depends. Some people have to pay for Medicare Part A coverage. Most must pay for Part B coverage unless they are eligible for the QMB or SLMB programs (see questions at the end of this chapter).

Whether or not you have to pay for Part A depends on how many quarters of coverage you have in covered employment for Social Security purposes. (Chapter 1 provides basic information about quarters of coverage.)

- You have premium-free enrollment in Part A if you have the forty quarters that are necessary for Social Security benefits.
- You pay a monthly premium of $183 (in 1995) for Part A if you have at least thirty quarters of employment in jobs covered by Social Security but not the forty quarters necessary to qualify for premium-free Part A enrollment.

- You pay a monthly premium of $261 (in 1995) for Part A if you have fewer than thirty quarters of coverage.

The cost of Medicare Part B coverage depends on when you enroll:

- The general premium for Medicare Part B is $46.10 per month (1995).
- If you do not enroll in the so-called "initial enrollment period" (discussed below), you will face higher premiums as a penalty for late enrollment.

ENROLLMENT

Where can I apply for Medicare?

You can file an application at the local Social Security district office. The same application can be used to apply for Social Security old age benefits and for Medicare. For the location of the nearest office, call 800-SSA-1213.

What is meant by the "initial enrollment period"?

Applications for Medicare generally are required to take place in a seven-month period known as the "initial enrollment period." This period includes the three months preceding the month of your sixty-fifth birthday, that month itself, and the following three months. For example, if you will turn 65 in June, your initial enrollment period begins on March 1 and ends on September 30.

What is meant by the "general enrollment period"?

The general enrollment period starts each year on January 1 and ends on March 31.

Are my Part B benefits affected if I don't enroll in the initial enrollment period?

Yes. The most advantageous time to apply for Part B is during the three-month period before the month when you turn 65 so that your coverage will start at age 65. If you apply during the month of your sixty-fifth birthday, or during the three-month period after that month, coverage will be delayed. And if you don't apply at all during the seven-month initial enrollment period, you will have to wait to enroll in Medicare Part B until the next general enrollment period, and your coverage will be delayed until July 1 of that year. In addition, you will have to pay a higher premium amount for Medicare Part B coverage due to a penalty imposed for late enrollment.

When should I enroll in Medicare Part A?

You can enroll in Medicare Part A at any time if you are entitled to premium-free coverage, and Part A coverage can be retroactive for up to six months.

However, if you have to pay for Part A coverage (because you do not meet the Social Security eligibility requirements), you must enroll during the initial enrollment period or the general enrollment period. If you wait until the general enrollment period to enroll in Part A, coverage will be delayed until July 1 of that year.

MEDICARE BENEFITS

Who is responsible for submitting claims to Medicare?

Generally, the providers of services, including physicians, medical supply companies, hospitals, nursing homes, and home care agencies, are responsible for submitting claim forms to Medicare. They cannot charge for the process of submitting claims.

Does Medicare cover all of my hospital care?

Medicare covers up to ninety days of care in hospitals. These ninety days are called a "benefit period." In 1995, you were responsible for paying $716 (a "deductible") for the first sixty days of hospital care and $179 per day (called "co-payments") for days 61 through 90 in each benefit period. You can be eligible for another ninety days of hospital care (another benefit period) each time you have been out of a hospital or skilled nursing facility for at least sixty continuous days. In addition, you have another sixty days of coverage that can be used once in your lifetime to extend a benefit period beyond ninety days (up to 150 days). In 1995, you had to pay $358 for each of these sixty days.

Are hospitals required to help me obtain services when I am being discharged?

Yes. Hospitals are supposed to work with you and your family to arrange for services you will need when you are discharged.

What is the Medicare coverage for nursing home care?

Medicare pays for up to 100 days per benefit period if you need "skilled" nursing care or rehabilitation services in nursing homes designated as skilled nursing facilities. Medicare pays for care in a nursing home, received for the first twenty days, as long as the care is "skilled" and provided daily. After the first twenty days, you are responsible for paying $89.50 per day (1995) for days 21 through 100. The services covered include registered and licensed practical nurses; physical, speech, and occupational therapy; and medications, supplies, and equipment.

What is meant by "skilled care"?

Skilled care is defined as services which are so complex that they can be performed only by (or under the supervision of) professional personnel, such as nurses or therapists.

What are Medicare's requirements for nursing home coverage?

In addition to requiring skilled nursing or rehabilitation services, you must also meet the following requirements in order to receive Medicare-covered care in a nursing home:
- you must have been hospitalized for at least three days prior to the nursing home stay;
- you must enter the nursing home within thirty days of leaving the hospital; and

- you must be treated in the nursing home for a condition that was treated in the hospital.

What coverage does Medicare provide if I need help at home?

Medicare's coverage of home care services is limited to nursing care; physical, speech, and occupational therapy; and home health aides, if you require "skilled" care (as defined above).

What are the Medicare eligibility requirements for home care?

In order to be eligible for Medicare-covered home care, you must:

(1) be homebound, that is, require assistance in order to leave your home;

(2) need skilled nursing care once a day for a predictable period of time, or at least once every sixty days;

(3) receive services in accordance with a physician's plan of care; and

(4) receive services from a Medicare-certified agency.

Medicare will *not* cover so-called unskilled services, such as those provided by a home attendant who cooks your meals, does your laundry, or helps you with bathing, dressing, or toileting.

How much home care will Medicare pay for?

If you meet the eligibility criteria listed above, Medicare will reimburse for up to thirty-five hours per week of nursing and home health aide services.

Does Medicare pay for medical equipment such as wheelchairs and canes?

Yes. Medicare helps pay for "durable medical equipment." That's defined as equipment that can be used again by other patients; serves a medical purpose; is generally useful only for people who are sick or injured; and is appropriate for use in the home.

Before Medicare will pay for durable medical equipment, a doctor must complete a form that documents why the equipment is needed. Furthermore, there are rules about how you must obtain the equipment if you want Medicare to pay. Some types of equipment must be rented, others must be purchased, and still other types may be either rented or purchased.

What benefits does Medicare cover for physician, medical, and surgical services?

Medicare pays 80 percent of a so-called "approved charge" after you have met an annual deductible of $100 (1995). If the provider (doctor or medical supply company) accepts "assignment," the provider is paid 80 percent of the approved charge directly by Medicare and you are responsible only for paying 20 percent of the approved charge.

What is meant by "assignment"?

When doctors accept assignment, they agree to accept Medicare's approved charge; they will not charge the patient more, and they will bill Medicare. However, if the provider does not accept assignment, you will be asked to pay the medical bill to the doctor, and Medicare will reimburse you for 80 percent of the approved charge. Providers who don't accept assignment may also charge more than the approved charge and, in that case, you would have more out-of-pocket costs.

Do all doctors or other providers accept assignment?

No, not all doctors accept assignment. Doctors that do accept assignment for all Medicare beneficiaries are called "participating providers." These doctors have signed an agreement to accept assignment for every Medicare patient they serve. They will be paid 80 percent of the approved charge directly by Medicare and can bill patients only for the remaining 20 percent. You can locate participating providers by requesting a list (at no charge) from the Medicare carrier or insurance company responsible for administering the Medicare Part B program in your state or county (see chapter 11).

Can doctors who are not participating providers accept assignment?

Yes. Those who have not agreed to be participating providers can still accept assignment for any patient they choose or on any individual claim they choose. To find out if your doctor accepts assignment, you should ask him or her prior to obtaining a medical service.

Are doctors limited in the amount they charge if they do not accept assignment?

Yes. Federal law limits the amount physicians who don't accept assignment can charge to 15 percent above the approved charge. For example, if Medicare approves $100

Medicare

for a visit to a doctor who does not accept assignment, the doctor can charge you no more than $115 (15% of $100 = $15; $100 + $15 = $115). Furthermore, some states have their own state rules on how much doctors can charge their Medicare beneficiaries. If you live in one of those states (listed in table 5-1), you should contact the appropriate office about the laws in your state.

TABLE 5-1
STATES WITH ASSIGNMENT LAWS

State	Agency
Connecticut	Connecticut Department of Social Services CONNMAP 25 Sigourney Street Hartford, CT 06106 800-443-9946 203-424-4925
Massachusetts	Executive Office of Elder Affairs 1 Ashburton Place Boston, MA 02108 800-882-2003 617-727-7750
Minnesota	Minnesota Board of Aging Office of the Ombudsman 444 Lafayette Road St. Paul, MN 55155-3843 800-657-3591
New York	State Office for the Aging 2 Empire State Plaza Albany, NY 12223 800-342-9871 518-474-5731

State	Agency
Ohio	Department of Health 246 North High Street P.O. Box 118 Columbus, OH 4326-0118 800-899-7127 614-466-2070
Pennsylvania	Department of Aging Market Street State Office Building 400 Market Street Harrisburg, PA 17101 717-783-8975
Rhode Island	Department of Elderly Affairs 160 Pine Street Providence, RI 02903-3708 800-322-2880 401-277-2880

Are there certain procedures that Medicare will cover only if the doctor accepts assignment?

Yes. When clinical diagnostic laboratory tests, such as blood tests and urinalysis, are conducted in doctors' offices, in hospital outpatient departments, or in independent clinical laboratories, Medicare will pay only if the claim is submitted on an assigned basis. For such claims, Medicare pays the provider 100 percent of an established amount and you do not have to pay anything. (In Maryland only, Medicare patients may be charged 20 percent for hospital outpatient tests.)

How can I find out how much Medicare will approve for a doctor's services?

You can ask your doctor ahead of time. Doctors and other service providers are sent a list of Medicare's approved charges by the insurance company which processes Medicare claims (known as a "carrier") at the beginning of each year. If the provider does not know his or her approved charge, you can call the Medicare Part B carrier yourself (see chapter 11 for the carrier in your state or county).

If you want to find out ahead of time, you will need to have the provider's name and the five-digit procedure code that the provider will submit for reimbursement to the carrier.

If the service has already been provided, you should review the Explanation of Medicare Benefits (EOMB) statement which the carrier sends you. It lists the provider's name, the date and type of service, the amount billed, and the amount approved by Medicare.

Does Medicare cover hospice care?

Yes. Medicare provides coverage for hospice services if you meet certain conditions:

- your attending physician and/or a physician associated with the hospice must certify that you are expected to die within six months;
- you must elect to receive hospice care and waive the right to certain other Medicare services not provided by the hospice; and
- the services must be provided by a Medicare-certified hospice program.

What is meant by hospice care?

Hospice care is care provided to patients with a terminal illness; it is meant to manage the illness rather than to cure it. Hospice care may include pain relief; nursing care; medical social services; physicians' services; counseling for you and your family; short-term inpatient care provided in a hospice, hospital, or skilled nursing facility; medical appliances and supplies; drugs; home care; and physical, occupational, and speech therapy. Hospice care can be rendered in the home, in a special designated hospice facility, in a separate part of a hospital, or in a nursing home.

How long can I receive hospice care?

You may receive hospice coverage for two periods of ninety days each, another period of thirty days, and one additional unlimited period of time. At the beginning of each period, your doctor must certify that you are terminally ill.

What other benefits are covered by Medicare?

Some other Medicare benefits are:
- screenings for breast cancer
- Pap smear screenings for early detection of cervical cancer
- flu, pneumococcal, and hepatitis B vaccines
- clinical psychologist services
- clinical social worker services
- anticancer drugs administered orally
- prosthetic devices (including cardiac pacemakers)

What services are not covered by Medicare?

Although Medicare covers a wide array of medical care, several important medical services that the elderly and the disabled may need are not covered. They include:

- routine physical examinations and tests
- most prescription drugs outside of the hospital
- dentures and most dental work
- eye examinations, eyeglasses, and contact lenses in most cases (Medicare will provide for one pair of eyeglasses after cataract surgery)
- hearing aids
- routine foot care (Medicare will pay, however, for therapeutic shoes and inserts for individuals with severe diabetic foot disease)
- cosmetic surgery

APPEALS

Does Medicare have an appeals system?

Yes. Like the Social Security program, Medicare also has a process to appeal decisions that you don't agree with. See the section on administrative appeals in chapter 1.

What types of issues can be appealed?

You can appeal a wide array of decisions made by your medical care provider. The basis for your appeal may include dissatisfaction with the quality of care you have received, the reimbursement rate you have received for medical care and services, denials of eligibility for services, and the amount of services you have been told you qualify for.

What can I do when I am not satisfied with the quality of care?

You can contact the Peer Review Organization (PRO) in your state (see chapter 11). PROs are made up of doctors and other health care professionals. They are paid by the federal government to review the care given to Medicare patients by hospitals, outpatient departments, skilled nursing facilities, home health agencies, ambulatory surgical centers, and certain health maintenance organizations. In some states, the health department also monitors the quality of care and receives complaints from patients.

What can I do if Medicare will not admit me to a hospital or will no longer pay for my stay in the hospital?

You should request a decision in writing and follow the instructions on how to appeal the decision. Also, you, a family member, or friend should contact the state or local office for the aging and request the name of a legal services or advocacy organization which assists on such matters. Lastly, you can contact the state Health Insurance Information, Counseling, and Assistance program (see chapter 11).

What can I do if a nursing home says that Medicare will not cover my care?

You can request that the nursing home submit a claim to Medicare and if Medicare denies the claim, this determination can be appealed. You will have sixty days from the date of the determination to appeal. As with appeals of hospital stays, legal assistance is recommended.

What can I do if the doctor has overcharged me?

You should contact the Medicare carrier which handles claims in your state or county. The carrier is listed on the EOMB statements. If you live in one of the states which has its own assignment laws, you should contact the organization listed in table 5-1.

What can I do if Medicare denies payment for doctor or related services or approves an inadequate amount of reimbursement?

You can request a review of the determination, which is similar to the request for reconsideration under Social Security and SSI claims. The EOMB statement will inform you to whom the appeal should be sent. You will have six months from the date on the EOMB statement to appeal the determination.

Where can I receive further information and assistance on the Medicare program?

You can contact the Health Insurance Information, Counseling, and Assistance programs listed in chapter 11.

AUXILIARY MEDICARE BENEFITS

What are the auxiliary benefits available to Medicare beneficiaries?

In addition to Medicare, there are a number of supplemental insurance options available to its beneficiaries that are outlined in chapter 7. You can also join a coordinated care plan, such as a health maintenance organization. In addition, there are two federal programs available for low income Medicare beneficiaries: the Qualified Medicare Beneficiary (QMB) program and the Specified Low Income Medicare Beneficiary (SLMB) program. Finally, if you are not eligible for the QMB and SLMB programs and you have a low income and limited savings, you may be eligible for the Medicaid program, described in chapter 6.

What is the "Qualified Medicare Beneficiary" program?

The QMB program pays the Medicare Part A and Part B premiums and certain deductibles and co-payments for doctor, hospital, and nursing home expenses which Medicare does not cover. To be eligible for QMB benefits, you must meet the QMB eligibility requirements for income and resources (see table 5-2).

TABLE 5-2
ELIGIBILITY REQUIREMENTS
FOR THE QMB PROGRAM, 1995

Beneficiary	Income limit (per month)	Resource limit	Burial set-aside
Individual	$642	$4,000	$1,500
Couple	$855	$6,000	$3,000

What is the "Specified Low Income Medicare Beneficiary" program?

The SLMB program pays only the Medicare Part B premium if your income is slightly higher than the QMB levels. To be eligible for SLMB in 1995, you had to meet the income and resource limits shown in table 5-3.

TABLE 5-3
ELIGIBILITY REQUIREMENTS
FOR THE SLMB PROGRAM, 1995

Beneficiary	Income limit (per month)	Resource limit	Burial set-aside
Individual	$643–$767	$4,000	$1,500
Couple	$856–$1,023	$6,000	$3,000

Where can I apply for the QMB and SLMB programs?

Applications for the QMB, SLMB, and Medicaid programs can be filed at the local Medicaid office in your area. To obtain the location of the local Medicaid office, you should contact your local office for the aging or a legal services program in your area. (See also chapter 11.)

Medicaid

Eligibility Requirements . . . Services and Benefits . . . Applying for Benefits . . . Dealing with Providers . . . Appeals.

Medicaid, enacted in 1965 at the same time as Medicare, is a "needs-based" medical assistance program for Americans who have very limited savings and low incomes. However, the Medicaid program does not provide medical coverage for all people who have limited incomes and resources; the Medicaid program primarily serves the elderly poor of 65 years and older; the disabled under 65; and the visually impaired under 65 years of age.

Although Medicaid was originally designed as a medical program for the very poor, its broad-based benefits also serve some other people. Because Medicaid, unlike Medicare, provides coverage for long-term care, such as nursing home and home care, middle class individuals are often forced to rely on its coverage for long-term care when their savings have been used up.

Medicaid is funded jointly by federal and state governments and is administered by the states through their own Medicaid programs. Federal Medicaid law requires that states provide certain basic services and allows states the option of providing other services. For that reason, the services covered by the Medicaid program vary dramatically from state to state.

This chapter provides a general overview of federal Medicaid requirements and mandated services and points out those areas which are variable from state to state. Individual and state-specific questions have to be referred to local Medicaid programs, which are listed in chapter 11.

ELIGIBILITY REQUIREMENTS

Can I be eligible for Medicaid if I am not a citizen of the United States?

Yes, if you are legally residing in the United States.

Can I be eligible for Medicaid if I am on Medicare or have other health insurance?

Yes. If you meet the income and resource requirements of the Medicaid program, you can be eligible for it even though you are also covered by Medicare or other health insurance. But Medicaid is the payor of last resort and will pay only for services that have not been covered by Medicare or your other health insurance.

Can I be eligible for Medicaid if I just moved from one state to another state?

Yes, if you intend to make the new state your home. Some states require a minimum time period for establishing residency. Examples of ways to demonstrate residency are:

- owning a home or leasing an apartment in the new state;
- prior residence or family presence in the new state;
- employment records, voter registration, driver's license, or tax returns for the new state; or
- having a bank account in the new state.

Can married couples be eligible for Medicaid?

Yes. Married couples are eligible for Medicaid if both are over 65, certified blind, or certified disabled and they have a combined monthly income and resources below the levels allowed in their state.

How do I know if I am eligible for Medicaid?

Medicaid does not cover all adults with low incomes and resources. In general, the following categories of people are eligible for Medicaid in most states if they have incomes at or below their state's monthly income level and resources at or below the amount determined by their state:

- 65 or over; certified blind (any age); or certified disabled (any age); or
- children, or adults caring for children, who are eligible for cash benefits under the Aid to Families with Dependent Children program.

A few states provide Medicaid for additional groups of people, such as childless adults who do not qualify for federal benefits but are receiving state welfare assistance.

How do I know if I am financially eligible for Medicaid?

Generally, states follow the Supplemental Security Income rules for income and resources (see also chapter 2). But for aged, blind, and disabled individuals who are not receiving SSI because their income and resources are above SSI levels, states are allowed to have less restrictive rules than the SSI rules.

What is meant by "income"?

Income is any recurring payment, including wages, pensions, Social Security, interest, dividends, and rent receipts. "In-kind" income, which is the value of food or shelter provided by another person, is also usually counted, although some states exempt it.

Are any kinds of income not counted by Medicaid?

Generally, the following kinds of income are exempt:
- the first $20 per month per household;
- the first $65 and one-half of the remainder of earned income;
- interest earned on burial fund accounts (as long as it remains in the burial account fund);
- foster care payments for an individual living in the home of the Medicaid recipient;
- federal disaster relief;

- support or maintenance payments, including home energy assistance, based on need, furnished by non-profit agencies or home energy suppliers or utilities;
- federal housing assistance; and
- German or Austrian war reparation payments for Holocaust survivors.

What is meant by "resources"?

Resources are any assets, including savings and checking accounts, stocks, bonds, life insurance policies, and real estate, wherever located, which can be converted into cash.

Are any resources not counted for Medicaid eligibility?

Yes. Generally, the following resources are not considered in determining Medicaid eligibility:
- clothing, furniture, personal effects, and acar;
- your home, as long as you are living in it;
- if you are institutionalized, your home, as long as you intend to return there;
- burial spaces;
- life insurance policies with no cash value; and
- a $1,500 burial fund account for yourself and one for your spouse.

Are resources held jointly with others counted when I apply for Medicaid?

Yes. Medicaid will count as a resource the portion of a joint bank account, jointly held securities, or jointly owned real estate which actually belongs to you under the laws of your state. If you have a joint bank account with your spouse, some states treat such accounts as owned half by each spouse. In other states, the amount belonging to each spouse depends on who contributed the money to the account.

I meet the resource limit for Medicaid, but my monthly income is greater than the amount my state allows. Can I still be eligible for Medicaid?

Some states have a program called the Surplus Income Program (or "spenddown" program) which allows monthly income in excess of the allowed amount to be offset by medical bills. In those states, if your income exceeds the allowed monthly income level, and if your monthly medical expenses exceed your excess income, you will be eligible for Medicaid each month after you have incurred medical expenses equal to your excess income. Medicaid will then cover the remainder of your medical expenses for the rest of the month.

For example, suppose the allowed Medicaid monthly income level for a single individual in your state is $300, you are single, and you have monthly income of $400. If your state has a Surplus Income Program, you will become eligible for Medicaid in any month in which you incur medical expenses of $100. Once you have shown your medical bill to Medicaid, you will then be eligible for the remainder of that month. In months when you have no medical expenses to offset your $100 surplus income amount, you will not be eligible for Medicaid.

My income is greater than the allowed monthly income level. I don't have large medical expenses, but I have very high rent expenses. Can I be eligible for the Surplus Income Program?

No, you are eligible for the Surplus Income Program only if your *medical* expenses are equal to or greater than your excess income.

I have more income or resources than my state allows. If I give away some income or resources, can I be eligible for Medicaid?

The answer depends on the type of services you need and the state you live in.

In most states, if you are applying for community or certain home care services, the answer is yes. That is, if you give away income or resources, you may be eligible for those Medicaid services, although Medicaid will ask you to show how and to whom you made the gifts.

However, if you are applying for institutional services, such as hospital or nursing home care, the answer in all states is no: you will not be eligible for Medicaid, at least not immediately. If you have given income or resources away, except to certain exempt individuals, within the thirty-six months preceding your application for Medicaid, you may be ineligible for institutional services for a period of time. The length of the ineligibility period, if any, depends on how much money you gave away, when you did so, and what state you live in.

Who are the exempt individuals to whom I can give income or resources without becoming ineligible for institutional services?

You will be eligible for institutional services, notwithstanding any transfers you have made, if the transfer was made to one of the following family members:

- your spouse
- your certified disabled or blind child of any age

In addition, you will be eligible for institutional services if you transferred your home to one of the following persons:

- a child under 21
- a sibling who has resided in your home for at least a year and has an ownership interest in the home
- an adult child who has resided in your home for two years and provided care which has allowed you to remain at home rather than going to a nursing home

Can my spouse give away income or resources if I am applying for Medicaid?

No. Any transfer by your spouse will be treated as though you made the transfer.

Can I transfer money to a trust and still be eligible for Medicaid?

It depends upon the provisions of the trust. It is important to consult a knowledgeable elder law attorney before giving away any money or establishing a trust.

I live in the community with my husband, who needs Medicaid services. We are not eligible for Medicaid as a couple, but he is eligible as an individual. Can he still receive Medicaid, or will my income and resources be counted as available to him?

Almost all states count one spouse's income and resources as available to the other spouse if neither spouse is in a nursing home. In a few states, however, one spouse can receive Medicaid services in the community or at home if that spouse meets the income and resource requirements for a single person and the nonapplying spouse refuses to provide income or resources toward the cost of the applying spouse's medical expenses. In these states, however, Medicaid has the right to sue the nonapplying spouse for contribution of income or resources. If you are in this situation, you should consult with a knowledgeable social worker and/or attorney.

MEDICAID SERVICES AND BENEFITS

What services for adults must be covered by Medicaid in all states?

The following services are mandated in all states:
- Physician services, including medical or surgical services furnished by a dentist if the service could also be furnished by a doctor
- Laboratory and X-ray services
- Rural health clinic services
- Transportation and other travel-related expenses to obtain necessary medical examinations and treatment

- Home health services, including part-time and intermittent nursing, medical supplies and equipment, and home health aide services (home health aides provide medically-related services, such as dressing changes, wound care, catheter or colostomy care, and other services which involve monitoring of an individual's illness or injury)
- Inpatient and outpatient hospital services
- Nursing home services (other than in mental institutions)

What other services for adults may be available under my state's Medicaid program?

The following services may be available:
- Clinic services given by or under the direction of a physician
- Home physical therapy, occupational therapy, speech pathology, and audiology services
- Private-duty nursing
- Hospice care, a program of combined home and institutional care for the terminally ill
- Dental services
- Physical therapy and related services
- Prescriptions drugs
- Dentures, prosthetic devices, and eyeglasses prescribed by either an ophthalmologist or optician
- Other rehabilitative services in an institution, at home, in a clinic, or at a practitioner's office
- Medical or remedial care recognized under state law and furnished by licensed practitioners, such as chiropractors

- Inpatient hospital, nursing home, or intermediate care facility services for individuals over 65 for mental disease
- Case management services
- Respiratory care services
- Personal care services at home (assistance with activities of daily living, such as bathing, dressing, eating, toileting, and walking, and housekeeping chores)
- Organ transplants
- Care in community-supported living arrangements for the developmentally disabled
- Alcohol and drug treatment

Are there any nonmedical services which states can provide under the Medicaid program?

Yes. Federal law allows states to apply for special permission ("waivers") to provide services that are not strictly medical. Some states have used waivers to provide adult day health programs; respite care which allows a family member caregiver time away from caring for the Medicaid patient; social work services; home-delivered or congregate meals; housekeeping; home repair and home maintenance; home alterations, such as ramps or widening of doorways; and transportation for nonmedical purposes, such as social events. Keep in mind that these kinds of services are often limited and may require separate application procedures. Check with your state Medicaid program for available options in your state.

How can I find out which services are available under Medicaid in my state?

You can call your state or local Medicaid office or your area Agency for Aging for information. Other reliable sources of information are knowledgeable social workers or attorneys working for legal services or specializing in elder law. A listing of these sources for information is provided in chapter 11.

Is there any limit to the number or amount of services that Medicaid will cover?

Generally, Medicaid must provide any number or amount of services that are "medically necessary." To contain costs, however, states use various methods to control the amount of services used. Some states require prior authorization for certain services, supplies, and equipment. For example, Medicaid may require that a written request for adult diapers, syringes, dressings, and other supplies be approved before a pharmacy can bill Medicaid for those items. Similarly, the purchase of durable medical equipment such as wheelchairs, walkers, shower stools, hearing aids, and orthopedic shoes may require prior approval by a Medicaid office.

In other states, Medicaid sets initial utilization limits for certain services. For example, an individual may be allowed six physician office visits a year, but need a doctor's authorization form to receive additional visits. Obtaining additional services in excess of these limits requires a doctor's order. States are also allowed to require second opinions for surgery and screen patients for medical necessity prior to admission to hospitals and nursing homes.

If my spouse must go to a nursing home on Medicaid, how much money can I keep to meet my expenses at home?

If one spouse must enter a nursing home and is eligible for Medicaid, the other spouse is allowed to keep some of the nursing home spouse's income to bring the income of the spouse in the community up to a certain income level, known as the "community spouse monthly maintenance needs allowance." This amount varies from state to state and was as low as $1,230 or as high as $1,870.50 per month in 1995. In addition, the community spouse is allowed to keep an amount of resources known as the "community spouse resource allowance." This amount also varies from state to state and was as low as $14,964 or as high as $74,820 in 1994.

Can Medicaid take money from my estate after I die if I received Medicaid services during my lifetime?

Yes. If you are over age 55 when you receive Medicaid services, Medicaid can claim reimbursement for the cost of those services from your estate unless your spouse or disabled or blind child is still living.

You should consult a knowledgeable elder law attorney if you wish to preserve your estate. In addition, your estate plan and your will should be reviewed by a knowledgeable elder law attorney when you apply for Medicaid.

APPLYING FOR BENEFITS

How do I apply for Medicaid?

You apply by filling out a written application form which you get from your local Medicaid office. You may bring someone to the Medicaid office to help you fill out your application. In many states, you do not have to fill out a separate application form if you are on SSI. If you are in the hospital or a nursing home, you can apply there.

What types of documentation do I need to apply for Medicaid?

To apply for Medicaid benefits, you need documents to verify the following facts about yourself:

- your age, if you are applying for Medicaid benefits on the basis of age
- your identity (passport, Social Security card, driver's license)
- your marital status (marriage certificate, divorce papers, spouse's death certificate)
- your place of residence (mortgage payment, lease, mail received at your home)
- your income (copies of your Social Security check, pension checks)
- your resources (all bankbooks, stock certificates, life insurance policies, certificates of deposit)
- any transfers of your income and resources within the last three years (checks, deeds)
- your disability, if you are applying as a disabled or visually impaired person

DEALING WITH PROVIDERS

Can I choose my own doctor or other health care provider if I am on Medicaid?

No. Medicaid will cover only the services of doctors and other providers who have agreed to accept Medicaid clients. Providers are not required to participate in the Medicaid program. You do have the right, however, to choose freely among providers participating in the Medicaid program unless your state has a "managed care plan" or HMO for delivering Medicaid-covered care, which limits you to certain providers affiliated with that plan.

If I use Medicaid providers or services, will I have to pay anything?

It depends. Some states charge co-payments for certain specific services. However, federal law requires that the co-payments be "minimal" and says that you cannot be denied goods or services if you cannot pay the co-payment amount before you receive the services. You can be billed, but the service cannot be denied.

Can a Medicaid provider charge me anything more than the provider is paid by Medicaid?

No. A Medicaid provider must accept the Medicaid payment as payment in full.

If my doctor doesn't take Medicaid, can I continue to see that doctor and use my Medicare card even after I am on Medicaid?

Yes, but you will have to pay the doctor the Medicare 20 percent co-payment unless you are covered by a Medicare Supplement Policy. Also, if the doctor does not accept Medicare assignment, you may have to pay an additional balance bill amount (see also chapters 5 and 7 on Medicare and Supplemental Medical Insurance).

How can I locate providers who participate in the Medicaid program?

You can call your state's Medicaid office. The information you receive, however, may not be current, so you should check with the provider before you receive services.

APPEALS

What can I do if Medicaid denies my application or reduces or terminates my services after I am on Medicaid?

You have the right to appeal any denial, reduction, or termination of Medicaid services. Each state's Medicaid program has its own appeals procedures. However, they have to comply with standard due process protections. Your right to due process includes the right to:

- submit an application, even if you are not sure whether you will be found eligible or not;
- receive a written notice from the Medicaid program about its decision concerning your eligibility;
- have an impartial hearing before the Medicaid agency to contest the decision if you don't agree with it;
- take additional steps to appeal any further decisions you don't agree with to higher authorities within the Medicaid program; and
- appeal the decision before a court of law.

CHAPTER

7

Supplemental Medical Insurance

Supplementing Medicare Coverage . . . Medigap Policies . . . Managed Care Plans . . . Obtaining Long-Term Care . . . Purchasing Long-Term Care Insurance . . . COBRA Coverage.

Supplemental medical insurance is a necessity for most Medicare recipients because of the many gaps in Medicare coverage. Medicare was designed in 1965 to meet the needs of older Americans who require acute care for an illness and who are expected to get better after having received skilled care for a short time in a hospital, in a nursing home, or at home. When Medicare was enacted, it was not created to address the needs of people with long-term illnesses or chronic conditions. As a result, Medicare falls far short of the goal of providing comprehensive medical care for the elderly.

Medicare does not cover two major areas of health care people over the age of 65 may need. Notable is the lack of coverage for preventive care and other routine health care, such as coverage for prescription drugs, hearing aids, dental care, eye care, and foot care. The other major gap in Medicare is the limited coverage for services required by individuals with chronic care conditions who need services for a long or an indefinite period of time. Such care, known as long-term care, is not covered by Medicare at all.

Today there are many options available to Medicare beneficiaries who wish to supplement Medicare to fill in some of the gaps in coverage. The options include: continuation in an employer plan; Medicare supplements, also called Medigap policies; managed or coordinated care plans; and long-term care insurance.

This chapter describes some of the options available to Medicare beneficiaries who wish to obtain supplements to Medicare or to purchase private insurance for long-term care.

SUPPLEMENTING MEDICARE COVERAGE

What are some of the gaps in Medicare coverage?

Medicare does not pay for many important items:

- certain deductibles and co-payments for Medicare-covered services (see chapter 5)
- charges above Medicare's approved charge (up to the limiting charge as outlined in chapter 5)
- preventive care
- prescription drugs
- hearing aids
- dental and eye care
- general foot care
- custodial care received at home or in a nursing home

Supplemental Medical Insurance

What options are available to fill in the gaps in Medicare coverage?

The following options are available to people 65 years old and over:

- Medicaid for people with low incomes and limited resources (see chapter 6)
- Qualified Medicare Beneficiary (QMB) program for people with low incomes and limited resources (see chapter 5)
- Specified Low Income Medicare Beneficiary (SLMB) program for people with low incomes and limited resources (see chapter 5)
- employer coverage
- Medicare supplement (or Medigap) health insurance
- managed care or coordinated care plans

Do I need additional coverage if I am on Medicaid or participate in the QMB program?

Medicare beneficiaries with low incomes and limited resources who are entitled to Medicaid or the QMB program usually do not need additional health insurance. In fact, it is against the law for an insurance company to sell a Medigap plan to a Medicaid recipient unless (1) the state or locality plans to pay the premiums or (2) Medicaid is not paying the full amounts of deductibles and co-payments faced by these low-income Medicare beneficiaries.

Individuals who already have a Medigap policy at the time they become eligible for Medicaid can suspend their Medigap coverage for up to two years (while they are on Medicaid), and if they once again become ineligible for

125

Medicaid benefits during that two-year period, they can renew their coverage under their prior Medigap plan.

MEDIGAP POLICIES

What is Medigap coverage?

Medigap, also called Medicare supplement health insurance, is a specific type of insurance designed to meet some of the expenses not covered or only partially covered by Medicare.

Who can purchase Medigap policies?

Medicare beneficiaries 65 and older are allowed to purchase any Medigap policy during a special "open enrollment" period, which is the six-month period after they first enroll in Medicare Part B. Disabled individuals who are eligible for Medicare prior to age 65 also have a six-month open enrollment period for purchasing a Medigap plan when they turn 65. During these six months, people cannot be denied Medigap insurance or charged higher premiums because of health problems. Some states may allow Medicare beneficiaries to enroll at other times; check with your state insurance department for the rules in your state (see chapter 11).

If I delay enrollment in Medicare Part B because I am covered by an employer health plan, will I be eligible for the six-month Medigap open enrollment period when I enroll in Medicare Part B?

Yes. If you delay enrollment in Medicare Part B because you are covered by your work health plan or your spouse's work plan, you will have a special seven-month enrollment period for Medicare Part B. It begins with the month your work or your spouse's work ends or when you are no longer covered under the employer plan, whichever comes first. Your six-month Medigap open enrollment period starts when your Part B coverage begins.

If I apply for a Medigap plan after the special six-month open enrollment period, can I be denied coverage?

Yes. In most states, companies can refuse to issue you a Medigap policy based on your health conditions except during the six-month open enrollment period.

What benefits are provided by Medigap health insurance policies?

The benefits provided by Medigap policies during 1995 are outlined in table 7-1. Most states allow insurance companies to offer only ten standard Medigap policies, identified as plans A through J. Plan A is known as a basic benefits plan. It covers the 20 percent co-payment for doctors' bills, the co-payments for hospital stays lasting more than sixty days, one year of hospital coverage in addition to Medicare's coverage, and the first three pints of blood. Plans B through J must contain the same benefits as plan A and provide additional benefits, which may include coverage for prescription drugs, limited home care, preventive care, and emergency care received outside of the country.

TABLE 7-1
MEDICARE SUPPLEMENT INSURANCE BENEFIT PLANS, 1995

MEDIGAP BENEFIT PLANS	BASIC Coverage 20% co-payment for doctors' bills; co-payment for hospital days 61-90 ($179/day); 91-150 ($358/day); plus 365 days over a lifetime; first three pints of blood.	Hospital Deductible ($716).	Skilled Nursing Facility copayment ($89.50/day for days 21-100)	Medicare Part B Deductible ($100/year).	Medicare Part B Charges in Excess of Medicare's Approved Charge (subject to federal and state limits).	Treatment outside of U.S.: 80% of emergency medical costs; $250 annual deductible and $50,000 lifetime benefits; care must begin within first two months of trip.	Home Care: Assistance with activities of daily living: up to 7 visits/week; maximum payment of $40/visit and $1,600 each year; conditioned upon receipt of Medicare home care benefits.	Drugs: Basic -- 50% of drugs subject to $250/year deductible and $1,250 annual limit.	Drugs: Extended -- 50% of drugs subject to $250/year deductible and $3,000 annual limit.	Preventive Care: flu shots; tests for diabetes, cancer and hearing disorders; annual physical; limit of $120/year.
PLAN 'A'	X									
PLAN 'B'	X	X								
PLAN 'C'	X	X	X	X		X				
PLAN 'D'	X	X	X			X	X			
PLAN 'E'	X	X	X			X				X
PLAN 'F'	X	X	X	X	X 100%	X				
PLAN 'G'	X	X	X		X 80%	X	X			
PLAN 'H'	X	X	X			X		X		
PLAN 'I'	X	X	X		X 100%	X	X	X		
PLAN 'J'	X	X	X	X	X 100%	X	X		X	X

Do all insurance companies offer Plans A through J?

Although each state must allow the sale of Plan A, insurance companies are not required to offer all of the other plans. Most offer several plans. Some states have limited the number of plans available.

Furthermore, residents of Minnesota, Massachusetts, and Wisconsin will find that the coverage of their Medigap plans differs from coverage under the ten standard plans. When Medigap was standardized in 1992, those states were allowed to continue to offer a few other kinds of plans.

If I previously purchased a Medigap policy which does not meet the requirements in Plans A through J, do I have to change policies?

Depending upon which state you live in, you may not have to switch to one of the ten standard Medigap plans if you have an older policy that is guaranteed renewable. "Guaranteed renewable" means that the insurance company cannot cancel or refuse to renew the policy unless the policyholder does not pay the premium or has made a "material misrepresentation" (such as providing incorrect information on the application). Persons who can retain their previous policies may still want to examine the benefits offered under Plans A through J to determine if they need additional benefits and want to replace their previous policies with one of Plans A through J.

Some states have specific requirements that affect existing nonstandard policies. For example, some states require or permit insurance companies to convert older policies to the standardized plans. Check with your state insurance department to find out what requirements apply in your state.

If I purchase one of Plans A through J, will I be covered for preexisting conditions?

It depends when you purchase it. If you are purchasing a Medigap plan for the first time, insurance companies are allowed to exclude coverage for preexisting conditions during the first six months the policy is in effect. (Preexisting conditions are conditions that were either diagnosed or treated during the six-month period before the Medigap policy became effective.) If you have had a Medigap policy for at least six months and you decide to switch, the new policy is not allowed to impose a waiting period for a preexisting condition if you satisfied a waiting period for a similar benefit under your old policy. If, however, a benefit is included in the new policy that was not included in the old policy, a waiting period of up to six months may be applied to that particular benefit. Check with your state insurance department, because some states have different rules.

If I have coverage under one of Plans A through J, can I purchase another Medigap plan?

No. Insurance companies are prohibited from selling you a Medigap policy if you already have one unless you indicate in writing that you intend to replace your prior Medigap policy with another one.

If I have Medicare and private health insurance from a former employer, should I consider purchasing a Medigap policy?

It depends on the benefits of your former employer's plan. Review the coverage and cost of that plan and compare it to the Medigap plans to determine if you need additional coverage.

After Medicare pays for a Part B service, does a claim have to be submitted to the beneficiary's Medigap company?

It depends on which provider performs the service and which Medigap company is insuring you. Most claims submitted by participating providers are automatically filed by the carrier with the Medigap company. Check with the Medicare carrier which handles claims for your area (see chapter 11).

How can individuals make informed decisions in selecting an appropriate Medigap policy?

First, they should review Medicare's benefits and gaps in coverage, which are outlined in chapter 5. Next, they should review the benefits offered in the Medigap plans available in their state (see table 7-1). Once they have decided which Medigap plan they want, they should obtain a list of companies with approved Medigap plans from their state insurance department. Then they should call some of the companies and request information on premiums of the Medigap plans which they have selected. In addition, they may want to contact their state health insurance counseling program to discuss which plan is appropriate for them.

Where can I obtain more information on Medigap policies in my state?

For a list of insurance companies offering Medigap coverage in your state and to obtain other information on these plans, contact your state insurance department (see chapter 11); for assistance on matters related to health insurance, contact your state health insurance counseling program (see chapter 11).

Medicare beneficiaries who are considering the purchase of private health insurance may want to review the "Guide to Health Insurance for People with Medicare" (#518B). For a free copy, contact your state office for aging or write to Consumer Information Center, Department 33, Pueblo, Colorado 81009.

What is the Medicare SELECT program?

Medicare SELECT is a type of Medigap insurance which is sold in Alabama, Arizona, California, Florida, Illinois, Indiana, Kentucky, Massachusetts, Minnesota, Missouri, North Dakota, Ohio, Texas, Washington, and Wisconsin. The difference between Medicare SELECT and standard Medigap insurance is that Medicare SELECT policies pay Medigap benefits only for items and services provided by certain selected health care professionals and facilities, or pay only partial benefits when you get health care from other health care providers. Medicare SELECT policies are expected to have lower premiums than standard Medigap policies because of this limitation.

MANAGED CARE PLANS

What is a managed care plan?

Managed care plans, also called coordinated care plans or prepaid plans, include health maintenance organizations (HMOs) and competitive medical plans. Managed care plans work with a network of physicians, hospitals, health centers, and other health care professionals to provide care to their members. These plans have contracts with Medicare to provide a full range of health care services to Medicare beneficiaries. In return, they receive money from Medicare for each Medicare beneficiary and they are allowed to charge enrollees a premium for their coverage and co-payments for their services. Contact your state insurance department for a list of Medicare HMOs in your state.

If I join a managed care plan, do I have to use the plan's network of health care providers?

It depends on the type of HMO you join.

If the HMO has a "risk" contract with Medicare, you must receive all your health care benefits (except for emergency or urgent care) from the HMO. If you obtain treatment from a non-HMO provider, neither the HMO nor Medicare will pay.

If you join a plan with a "cost" contract with Medicare, you can receive covered services outside the HMO. If you obtain services from outside the HMO, Medicare pays and you are responsible for Medicare's deductibles and coinsurance.

Who is eligible to enroll in a Medicare-managed care plan?

In general, you are eligible to enroll in a Medicare-managed care plan if you are enrolled in Medicare Part B and live in the plan's service area. However, you will be ineligible if you have permanent kidney failure or have selected the Medicare hospice benefit.

What are the advantages of enrolling in a Medicare HMO?

The advantages of joining a Medicare HMO plan include the following:

- Some Medicare HMOs provide benefits beyond what Medicare covers, including preventive care, prescription drugs, dental care, hearing aids, eyeglasses, and routine foot care.
- Members do not have to pay the Medicare deductible and co-payments.
- Both disabled and aged Medicare beneficiaries generally may enroll in Medicare HMOs without regard to any health problems they have (except for those with certain conditions mentioned earlier).
- Enrollees are better able to budget for health care expenses because their out-of-pocket expenses are minimal.
- Members do not have to file claims with Medigap or other private insurance companies.

What are some of the disadvantages of joining a Medicare HMO?

Risk-contract HMOs may not be appropriate for people who feel attached to particular physicians or health facilities not associated with an HMO and who want to be able to utilize nonaffiliated providers. Also, those who plan to spend long periods of time outside of the HMO service area should not choose this option. Lastly, the appeals process for Medicare beneficiaries in HMOs tends to take longer than for beneficiaries not in HMOs.

If I enroll in a Medicare HMO, can I disenroll at a later date?

Yes. Members may disenroll from an HMO at any time by sending a request to the HMO or to their local Social Security Administration office. Regular Medicare benefits will resume the first day of the month following the month a termination request is received. Medicare beneficiaries may also disenroll from a Medicare HMO and join a different HMO.

If I am enrolled in a Medicare HMO can I also purchase Medigap coverage?

No. Medigap insurance is not allowed to be offered to members of Medicare HMOs, because it is considered duplicate coverage.

Should I select my employer's retirement health plan to supplement Medicare?

It depends on the coverage provided by the employer plan. You should compare the benefits and cost of the plan with Medigap policies and managed care plans.

OBTAINING LONG-TERM CARE

What is long-term care?

Long-term care includes a wide range of medical and nonmedical services designed to meet the needs of people who are expected to require assistance over a long period of time. This care often includes help with bathing, dressing, walking, eating, cooking, and other activities. Long-term care can be provided at home, in a nursing home, in a rehabilitation facility, or in another setting such as an adult day program.

Is long-term care similar to hospital care?

No. People in hospitals usually receive the services of a doctor, nurse, or other skilled health care professional to help them recover from an illness or an injury. Their condition is expected to improve in a relatively short period of time. In contrast, long-term care is provided to people who suffer from a lingering illness, such as a stroke, and who will require care indefinitely. Some people may require both hospital care and long-term care, as in the case of a person who suffers a broken hip.

What services are included in long-term care?

The following medical and nonmedical services are included in the definition of long-term care:

- Custodial services (including light housekeeping, laundry, shopping, paying bills, home-delivered meals, and personal care services such as bathing, grooming, and dressing)

- Health-related services (including nursing, dressing changes, wound care, catheter and colostomy care, and physical, speech, and occupational therapy)
- Adult day programs (which may provide social activities, supervision, monitoring, personal care, nutrition, transportation, and medical care)
- Respite programs (which provide care to dependent individuals for a short time, allowing regular caregivers a rest from their responsibilities)

How much does long-term care cost?

Long-term care services provided by nursing homes for individuals who pay privately varies depending upon which part of the country you reside in. National estimates are that nursing home care costs about $30,000 a year, but in some urban areas it can be over $80,000 a year. Home care, depending upon the type and amount of assistance required, usually is less expensive than a nursing home, but can cost more than nursing home care if long hours and/or highly skilled services are required. Home care assistance for custodial needs costs about $8 to $15 per hour (depending upon region).

Does Medicare cover the cost of long-term care?

Medicare provides limited coverage for care delivered at home or in a nursing home. To obtain Medicare coverage for home care services, the patient must need skilled care — services so complex that they can be performed only by professional personnel, such as nurses and therapists. People who meet the strict Medicare criteria usually get home care for only a short period of time. Most people at home or in a nursing home do not require skilled care but instead require custodial care — assistance with dressing, bathing, and eating. This type of care is covered by Medicare only if it is provided in addition to skilled care. Medicare does not provide coverage for someone requiring only custodial care.

Do Medigap policies or Medicare HMOs cover long-term care?

No. Neither Medigap policies nor Medicare HMOs provide benefits for individuals receiving custodial care in nursing homes or at home. Some of the Medigap plans provide limited assistance with activities of daily living (such as eating, dressing, bathing) for individuals who also receive skilled home care services covered by Medicare.

Will Medicaid pay for long-term care?

Yes. Medicaid, a government health care program for the elderly and disabled, pays for nursing home care and in a few states for home care (see chapter 6).

Who provides long-term care services?

Depending on whether the care is skilled (medical) or nonskilled (nonmedical), a variety of agencies may provide some form of long-term care service.

County departments of social services may provide skilled and nonskilled services funded by Medicaid or other state and local programs.

Certified home health agencies provide skilled nursing services and physical, speech, and occupational therapy through Medicare, Medicaid, and private pay.

Private home care agencies (in some states known as licensed home care services agencies) provide assistance with bathing, grooming, and housekeeping through private pay.

Other organizations such as health departments, senior centers, hospitals, adult homes, and nursing homes (which are paid through various funding sources) may also provide long-term care.

PURCHASING LONG-TERM CARE INSURANCE

Will private insurance policies cover long-term care expenses?

Yes. A number of private insurance companies sell policies which cover some portion of long-term care expenses. Contact your state insurance department for a list of such companies.

What is the cost of long-term care policies?

The cost varies depending upon the age of the applicant, the benefits chosen, and the insurance company selected. Check with your state insurance department for information on premiums.

What factors should be considered before purchasing long-term care insurance?

If you wish to purchase long-term care insurance, you should evaluate the following factors:

- Your financial situation. Determine how much income and savings you will have in the future to pay for long-term care at the time you may need it. If you have relatively little savings and a low income, you may qualify for the Medicaid program after a short time of paying privately. In that case, purchasing private insurance may be unnecessary.

- Your family arrangements. Talk with family members about their ability and willingness to care for you if you need home care or nursing home care. Can you expect to be cared for by your family for both short and long periods of time? Do you have family nearby or are they willing to move? Can the family afford to pay for someone else to provide assistance?
- Your health. Do you have any health problems which may require long-term care services soon? While this may seem like a good reason to purchase private insurance, many companies won't insure someone in poor health. If you are in good health, you should consider purchasing long-term care insurance while you can.
- Your family history. While predicting whether you will require long-term care in the future is impossible, a family history of certain diseases, such as heart disease or Alzheimer's disease, may indicate that you are at greater risk of needing long-term care.
- Your age. The younger you are when you purchase a policy, the lower the cost. Premiums become more expensive for older persons who purchase a policy. Furthermore, most companies will not issue policies to people who are older than a certain age, such as 80.

What other options are available for covering long-term care expenses?

Some states, including New York, Connecticut, California, and Indiana, have started a public-private partnership program between the state Medicaid program and selected private insurance companies to help pay for long-term care expenses. While each state differs as to how the program operates, the purpose is to offer coverage for long-term care services through private insurance companies so individuals will not have to impoverish themselves and then rely solely upon Medicaid for long-term care expenses. Under this program, you can purchase certain state-approved long-term care insurance policies; then, once you have used up the private benefits, you can become eligible for Medicaid and keep more assets than Medicaid allows for individuals who are not part of the partnership program. If you live in a state that has such a program, check with your state insurance department for more information. (If you live in another state, contact your state insurance department for information on other options.)

Which provisions of long-term care policies should be examined before purchasing such policies?

A complete list of questions that you should ask about long-term care policies is provided in the appendix at the end of this chapter (Checklist for Purchasing Long-Term Care Insurance Policies).

Where can I obtain help to evaluate long-term care policies?

For assistance in evaluating long-term care insurance policies, call your state health insurance counseling program (see chapter 11). You can also request a copy of "A Shopper's Guide to Long-Term Care Insurance" from your state insurance department or from the National Association of Insurance Commissioners, 120 West 12th Street, Suite 1100, Kansas City, MO 64105-1925.

COBRA COVERAGE

I am under 65 years of age and have lost my employee health insurance. What can I do?

Under a federal law known as COBRA (Consolidated Omnibus Budget Reconciliation Act), employers who have a group health plan and employ twenty or more workers must offer health insurance to workers, spouses, and dependent children who lose their health coverage due to certain "qualifying events." The qualifying events include:

- termination of employment (other than for gross misconduct);
- reduction in hours of employment;
- death of the covered employee;
- divorce or legal separation of the covered employee;
- the covered employee's entitlement to Medicare; and
- a child's losing dependent status.

How long can I continue my work health plan?

If termination or reduction in hours is the qualifying event, health insurance coverage must last at least eighteen months. For other qualifying events, the period of coverage must extend for thirty-six months (see table 7-2). Special rules for disabled individuals may extend the maximum periods of coverage.

Although COBRA specifies certain maximum required periods of time that continued health coverage must be offered, companies can offer coverage in addition to these periods and some plans allow beneficiaries to convert group health coverage to an individual policy.

Will my coverage under COBRA be the same as I had before?

Yes. Beneficiaries must be offered health benefits identical to those they were receiving immediately before they qualified for COBRA health insurance coverage.

How much will it cost to continue health insurance coverage under COBRA?

Beneficiaries may be required to pay the entire premium for coverage. The premium can be based upon the total cost of group health coverage, including the portion paid by employees and any portion paid by the employer for similarly situated active employees, plus 2 percent for administrative costs.

TABLE 7-2
PERIODS OF COBRA COVERAGE

Qualifying event	Beneficiary	Coverage
Termination of employment	Employee, spouse, and dependent children	18 months
Reduction of hours	Employee, spouse, and dependent children	18 months
Employee entitled to Medicare	Spouse and dependent children	36 months
Divorce or legal seperation	Spouse and dependent children	36 months
Death of covered employee	Spouse and dependent children	36 months
Loss of "dependent child" status	Dependent child	36 months

Where can I get more information?

For further information on COBRA, contact:

Older Women's League
666 11th Street, N.W., Suite 700
Washington, D.C. 20001
Telephone: 202-783-6686

If you are not eligible for continued health benefits under COBRA because your former employer has fewer than twenty workers, you may still have some protection under state laws. Check with your state insurance department for more information.

APPENDIX

CHECKLIST FOR PURCHASING LONG-TERM CARE INSURANCE POLICIES

EXCLUSIONS:

Are certain health conditions not covered (i.e., mental illness, depression)?
* Do you have any of these conditions?

PREEXISTING CONDITIONS:

Does the policy state that you won't be covered for preexisting conditions until a certain period of time after the policy has started?
* Do you have any of these conditions?
* How long is this period of time?

NURSING HOME COVERAGE:

Does the policy cover nursing home care?
* Which levels of nursing home care?
* What are the eligibility criteria for each level of nursing home care?
* Waiting Period: How many days must you pay out-of-pocket before the policy will cover care?
* Benefit: How much will the policy pay per day for each level of nursing home care?
* How does this amount compare with average nursing home costs in your community?
* What is the maximum number of days payable for nursing home care?

- What is the maximum amount paid for nursing home care?
- How is a benefit period defined?
- Is there a waiting period for each benefit period?
- How long is this period?

HOME CARE COVERAGE:

Does the policy cover home care?
- Which types of home care are covered?
- Are these home care services available in your community?
- What are the eligibility criteria for each type of home care?
- Waiting Period: How many days must you pay out-of-pocket before the policy will cover care?
- Benefit: How much will the policy pay per day for each type of home care?
- How does this amount compare with average home care costs in your community?
- What is the maximum number of days payable for each type of care?
- What is the maximum amount paid for each type of care?
- How is a benefit period defined?
- Is there a waiting period for each benefit period?
- How long is this period?

OTHER BENEFITS:

Does the policy pay for any other services (such as, for instance, adult day care)?

- Under what conditions will the policy cover this other type of care?
- For how long is the coverage?
- How much does the policy pay?

GATEKEEPER:

Who determines the number of hours and types of services you require?

- Can this determination be appealed?

TYPE OF SERVICE PROVIDER:

Does the policy require that nursing home or home care must be provided by certain types of facilities or agencies, such as those which are state- or Medicare-certified or those which have a contract with the insurance company?

- Are these facilities or home care agencies available in your community?

COST:

What are the premiums?

- Can they be increased?
- Under what conditions?
- Is there a provision that premiums don't have to be paid after benefits are provided for a certain period of time?
- How long is this period?

RENEWABILITY:

Can the policy be canceled?
  • Under what conditions?

POLICY EXAMINATION:

Is there a period during which you are allowed to examine the policy and return it without being charged?
  • How long is this period?

ASSISTANCE:

Is there a toll-free number to call for general information and claims assistance?

INFLATION PROTECTION:

Does the policy offer the option of automatic increases in benefits to keep pace with inflation?
  • How is it computed?
  • Does this option have to be selected when the policy is initially purchased or can it be selected at a future date?
  • What is the charge for this provision?

LIMITS ON SERVICE AREA:

Does the policy pay for benefits only if you reside in a certain service area?
  • How will this affect you?

EXTENSION OF BENEFITS:

Will the policy continue to pay benefits if you have exhausted all benefits while receiving care which the policy covers?
  •Under what conditions and for how long?

POLICY UPGRADE:

Are you allowed to purchase improved benefits should such coverage be offered by the insurance company?
  • If so, under what conditions?

NONFORFEITURE BENEFITS:

Does the insurance company provide for reduced benefits if your policy lapses after a specified number of years?

FINANCIAL STABILITY OF INSURANCE COMPANY:

Is the company financially stable?
  • What rating has A.M. Best Company or Standard and Poor's assigned to your insurance company?

PAST EXPERIENCE:

Does the company have a history of consumer complaints or abuses in the long-term care insurance or Medigap market? (You may wish to contact your state insurance department.)

CHAPTER

8

Home Care and Other Community- Based Services

What is Home Care? . . . Medicare Home Care Services . . . Medicaid Home Care Services . . . Other Ways to Pay for Home Care . . . Enforcing Your Rights.

As people become older, their chronic medical conditions and other physical frailties may well get worse. It may no longer be possible for them to live on their own without help. But the vast majority of older or disabled people in that situation wish to stay in their own homes and to avoid moving to a nursing home. In recognition of the need and people's preferences, there are now alternatives to nursing homes or other institutions for people who need help with the normal activities of daily living.

Home care and other community-based services can provide the support that allows older or disabled people to

151

remain in their own homes and communities. Home care consists of a variety of medical and nonmedical support services, from skilled nursing and therapies to personal care and housekeeping. Other community-based services may include meals on wheels, escort services, telephone reassurance programs, and respite care for family members.

Funding for home care comes from a wide variety of federal, state, public, and private sources. It is limited by factors such as the nature of the patient's illness or frailty; whether the patient needs medical or custodial care; whether the patient can give direction to the home care workers; whether there are family members or other caregivers involved; to what extent the home care will be needed on a long-term or short-term basis; entitlement to Medicare and Medicaid; availability of private insurance; and the financial situation of the patient.

This chapter describes various types of home care and other community-based services that may be available to help older and disabled people remain in the community rather than in nursing homes or other institutions.

WHAT IS HOME CARE?

What kinds of medical services are available at home?

The medical home care services available to older people or the disabled include:

- high-tech services (intravenous drug therapy, artificial feeding and hydration, kidney dialysis, and oxygen therapy)

- part-time nursing (wound care, injections, catheter and colostomy care, administration of medication, and other services requiring the skills of a nurse)
- private duty nursing
- home health aide services
- audiology, respiratory therapy, and physical, speech, and occupational rehabilitation and maintenance visits

What are home health aide services?

Home health aide services are services that require special training to perform. They are related to medical matters. Depending upon your state's professional licensing laws, home health aides may be able to change dressings on stable surface wounds, apply certain skin treatments, foot soaks, and heat treatments, monitor vital signs such as temperature and blood pressure, prepare special diets, perform routine catheter and colostomy care, suction individuals with stable tracheotomies, and monitor unstable medical conditions.

What are personal care services?

As compared with home health aide services, personal care services (also called personal assistance) are generally considered less medical. Personal care is provided for individuals whose medical condition is stable and does not require the monitoring skills of a trained home health aide. (A home health aide may provide personal care services in addition to home health aide services for particular individuals who need both.) Personal care involves help with what are known as activities of daily living. These activities, often referred to as ADLs, include hands-on assistance with bathing, dressing, grooming, eating, walking, toileting, and transferring from bed or chair to wheelchair.

What are housekeeper/chore services?

Housekeeper/chore services, also known as instrumental activities of daily living or IADLs, include assistance with cooking, shopping, cleaning, and laundry.

Are any other kinds of services available at home?

Yes. Other kinds of support services, such as home-delivered meals, personal emergency response systems, assistance with home maintenance tasks and repairs, home modifications, such as ramps, widening of doorways and installation of safety railings, yard work, driving, care of pets, bill paying, and bookkeeping, may also be available.

What are personal emergency response systems?

A personal emergency response system, also called PERS, involves an electronic gadget that is hooked up to your telephone. PERS has several additional components:

- a call button you wear on your person that can be activated wherever and whenever you need it in an emergency (for example, a fall in the bathroom);
- a central monitoring system that is staffed twenty-four hours a day to receive emergency calls and respond; and
- a person you designate to be called by the central number in case of an emergency.

What are community-based services?

Community-based services are services provided outside the home to assist you or family members or friends who are helping you at home. Community-based services include congregate meals (at a senior center or other location where older persons get together), respite care (either at home or in an institution, to give family or friends a break from assisting you), transportation, social or medical day care, telephone reassurance, friendly visiting, and educational and recreational activities. These services are usually an integral part of a home care plan.

Are all of these services available in every state?

If you can afford to pay privately, you will be able to purchase most of the services mentioned above in most states, although more services are typically available in urban and suburban areas than in rural areas. If you cannot afford to pay privately, the kinds and amounts of publicly funded services vary dramatically from state to state. In some states, very few publicly funded home and community-based services are available.

What kind of agencies provide home care services?

Certified agencies usually provide medical home care services. "Certified" generally means that the agency is certified under the Medicare and Medicaid programs to receive payment from those programs. Certified home care agencies must meet federally mandated requirements. They typically offer skilled home care services, such as nursing, home health aide services, and the skilled therapy services — physical, speech, and occupational therapy. Some certified agencies now also offer the so-called high-tech home care services, such as intravenous medication and artificial tube feeding.

What is a personal care provider?

A personal care provider may be an individual or an agency. Agencies which furnish only personal care services are not certified, because they do not offer the skilled services which Medicare and Medicaid require. Some states require that home care agencies that are not certified must be licensed by the state. Personal care providers may contract with certified agencies to provide personal care services to clients for whom the certified agency is providing skilled home care services funded by Medicare and/or Medicaid. Some state Medicaid programs contract directly with personal care providers if they have opted to provide these services under the state plan.

What are nursing agencies?

A nursing agency provides private duty nurses to individuals wishing to pay for this service. Some states also cover private duty nursing under their state Medicaid programs. In those states, nurses who wish to participate in the Medicaid program usually function as individual providers and bill Medicaid directly for their services.

What is a hospice program?

A hospice program provides care for individuals with terminal illness who agree to accept palliative or comfort care but forgo active medical treatment. Hospice care combines home and institutional services, but most of the services are generally given at home, and most patients in hospice programs die at home. Hospice programs usually require a significant commitment to caregiving by family members and other informal caregivers. Services include nursing, personal care, counseling for family members, and pastoral care.

Hospice care is covered under Medicare (see discussion in chapter 5) and is an optional service for the states under Medicaid.

How can I find out which kinds of home and community-based services are available in my state?

You can call your state or local office for the aging. Chapter 11 lists the offices for the aging for all fifty states. You can apply directly to a certified home care agency, a personal care provider, a nursing agency, or a hospice program or you can ask a social worker in a community social service agency, a senior center, a hospital, or a nursing home. Some social workers, called geriatric care managers, also practice privately. The National Association of Professional Geriatric Care Managers is listed in chapter 11.

What kinds of expenses will I have for home care services?

The cost of each service generally depends upon the level of skill needed to perform the task and how long the task takes. Visits by skilled professionals, such as nurses and therapists, are the most expensive and are usually billed by the visit. Less skilled services, such as personal care or chore services, cost less and are usually billed by the hour.

In addition to the costs for the worker who visits your home, you may need to buy or rent special durable medical equipment (such as a cane, a walker, a wheelchair, a bathing chair or bench, a commode, a seat lift chair, a lift from the bed, or a hospital bed). You may also need to buy supplies (such as adult diapers, catheter or colostomy supplies, needles for injections, or bed pads).

Are home care services more expensive than nursing home services?

Usually home care services are less expensive than nursing home services, but remember that you will still have all the expenses of maintaining your home and purchasing food if you remain at home. If you need many skilled services and many hours of personal care, your home care could cost more than nursing home care.

What kinds of public funding cover home care services?

Medicare and Medicaid cover some skilled medical home care services. In addition, some states cover personal care and other home care services as well as a limited amount of home and community-based services under their Medicaid programs (see discussion below). Limited amounts of federal funding are also available under the Older Americans Act, Social Service Block Grants, and Veterans Administration programs. Some states supplement these federal funds with general state revenue funds for home care programs. The kinds of services available and the mix of funding for them vary dramatically from state to state.

Can I receive home care if I live alone?

This depends upon the ability and willingness of family members and friends to assist you, your capacity to direct your home care workers, and your preference about remaining in your own home or moving to a group setting where more socializing is available.

MEDICARE HOME CARE SERVICES

What are the eligibility rules for Medicare home care?

A Medicare-enrolled person who is homebound because of an illness or injury and needs medical treatment or therapy may qualify for part-time, skilled health care services at home. You must meet all of the following conditions to qualify for Medicare coverage of home health care:

(1) A physician must certify the need for the services.

(2) You must be under the care of a physician who periodically reviews your treatment plan.

(3) You must be receiving *skilled* care, which may be any one of the following: skilled nursing care that is less than full time; or physical therapy; or speech therapy; or occupational therapy that you receive after having received speech or physical therapy that has ended.

(4) You must be "homebound" — in other words, unable to leave the home because of illness or

159

injury without the assistance of a person or device and without a considerable and taxing effort. (Trips from the home for medical reasons or short and infrequent trips for nonmedical purposes are acceptable if all of the other requirements of the definition are met.)

(5) The home health agency providing services must be certified by Medicare.

What home care services does Medicare cover?

If all five of the above conditions are met, Medicare will pay for the following home health services:

- combined skilled nursing and home health aide services which are "part-time" or "intermittent" for no more than thirty-five hours a week, except that fifty-six hours a week may be allowed for a short period of time such as two or three weeks
- physical therapy
- speech therapy
- occupational therapy
- medical social work, supervised by a physician
- medical supplies and equipment

What home care services are not covered by Medicare?

The following services are not covered by Medicare:

- drugs (except immunosuppressive drugs)
- meals delivered to the home
- homemaker or chore services, unless they are incidental to patient care

Do I have to pay a deductible or co-insurance amount for Medicare-covered home care services?

No. There is no deductible or co-payment amount for Medicare home care services, but Congress is currently considering proposals to impose co-payments and deductibles on this benefit.

Can I get Medicare home care services if I was not hospitalized before applying?

Yes. Unlike Medicare coverage of nursing home care, Medicare coverage of home health care doesn't require a three-day prior hospitalization. Many doctors, nurses, and social workers may not know this and may erroneously tell you that you cannot receive Medicare coverage of your home care because you were not hospitalized.

Where do I apply for Medicare-covered home care?

You must apply to a Medicare-certified home care agency. The agency will make a home visit and evaluate your care needs. Then the agency decides, based on the best professional judgment of its staff, whether Medicare will cover your care.

Is the agency's decision binding on Medicare?

No. The decision of the agency is not an official Medicare determination, and it may be wrong. The rules for Medicare coverage of home care services are complex. Even some Medicare-certified home health agencies may not understand the rules completely and may make an incorrect judgment about your situation.

What should I do if the certified agency tells me that Medicare will not cover my care?

If a certified agency tells you that Medicare will not cover your home care, you have the right to demand that the agency provide services to you and submit the bill to Medicare. You will not have to pay the agency until Medicare makes a coverage decision. If Medicare denies coverage, you will then have to pay privately for the services you received from the agency, but you will also have gained the right to appeal the Medicare coverage denial. Many Medicare home health care denials are reversed on appeal.

How do I appeal a Medicare denial?

The Medicare appeals process is discussed in chapter 5. If you have questions about your rights to Medicare home health coverage, call the Medicare advocacy organization in your state, your state office for the aging, or your state's health insurance counseling project. These organizations are listed in chapter 11. You can also call a legal services program in your area or an elder law attorney in private practice.

MEDICAID HOME CARE SERVICES

Does Medicaid cover home care services?

Yes. If you are eligible for Medicaid (see chapter 6 for more information about Medicaid eligibility), you will be able to obtain some home care services. The Medicaid rules for home care eligibility are much less stringent than the Medicare rules. For example, Medicaid does not require that you be homebound, that you be receiving a skilled service before other home care services are covered, or that your care be received from a certified agency.

What home care services must be covered under Medicaid in all states?

Mandatory medical home health services must be covered by Medicaid in all states. These services have to be prescribed by the client's physician and provided by a certified agency. The services include:

- part-time or intermittent nursing care
- home health aide services
- medical supplies and equipment

Although these services must be offered, federal law does not say how much of these services must be provided. States usually set a visit limit or a dollar limit on medical home health services. Also, they generally require that you file a special application for approval by the state Medicaid office before you can receive these services.

Does Medicaid cover any other skilled home health services?

Yes, in some states. States have the option of providing private duty nursing, physical therapy, occupational therapy, speech pathology, respiratory therapy for certain ventilator-dependent individuals, and audiology services at home. Most states provide physical, speech, and occupational therapy services. Fewer states provide private duty nursing.

Does Medicaid cover personal care?

Again, it depends on where you live. States have the option to provide personal care services under their Medicaid programs. Thirty-two states cover personal care, although the amount of personal care available varies widely from state to state.

Does Medicaid cover any other home and community-based services?

Yes. States can apply for special programs, called home and community-based waiver programs, which allow them to be creative in giving services not strictly medical to enable individuals to remain in the community rather than enter a nursing home. As of July 1993, forty-six states had waiver programs serving the elderly. The jurisdictions without such waivers were Arizona, the District of Columbia, Oklahoma, Pennsylvania, and Texas.

Where do I apply for Medicaid-covered home care services?

In most states, the department of social services administers the Medicaid program; in some states, it may be the state office for the aging or the health department. Call your state Medicaid agency or local office for the aging to find out where to apply. Telephone numbers for these agencies are listed in chapter 11.

OTHER WAYS TO PAY FOR HOME CARE

Are there other publicly funded home care programs besides Medicare and Medicaid?

Yes. Most states have limited programs funded with a combination of other federal and state funds. Generally these programs are administered by the state office on aging. These programs often seek to serve individuals who are just above Medicaid financial eligibility levels. They may provide services on a sliding fee scale and may also provide services generally not available under Medicaid programs, such as respite services, home repair and home modification, social day care, and transportation to social activities.

Do employee health insurance plans cover home care?

Generally, coverage for home care services is very limited in employee or retiree health insurance plans. If you have such a plan, check with your employer's benefit office and ask for a copy of the plan description. Do not assume that the information you receive on the telephone is correct.

Does Medicare Supplement Insurance (Medigap) cover home care services?

Of the ten standard Medicare Supplement insurance policies (discussed in chapter 7), only Plans D, G, I, and J contain any coverage for home care services. These plans cover only assistance with the activities of daily living up to seven visits per week; there is a maximum payment of

$40 per visit and a total limit of $1,600 per year if the patient is receiving Medicare-covered home care services.

Does private long-term care insurance cover home care services?

Some long-term care policies cover limited amounts of home care services. (See also chapter 7.)

What should I do if I want to hire my own home care worker and pay privately?

Make sure that you have a written agreement with the individual worker (or agency if one is involved). It should cover the tasks to be performed by the worker, the hours of work, salary and times of payment, sick time and vacations, and particular conduct that you will not allow, such as smoking, lateness, and intoxication. The agreement should also specify how unavoidable absences or sickness will be covered and who is responsible for providing replacement workers. If you are hiring an individual, remember that you must file the necessary income tax and other forms required for household employees.

ENFORCING YOUR RIGHTS

What should I do if I am not satisfied with the home care services I am receiving?

First, negotiate with the worker or the agency to resolve the problem. If no resolution is possible, many states have long-term-care ombudsman programs which will assist you by investigating and mediating your complaint. If the agency is licensed by your state or certified by Medicare or Medicaid, there is likely to be a consumer complaint telephone number where you can file a report and trigger an investigation.

What are my rights and responsibilities as a home care recipient?

Some states have developed a list of the rights of home care recipients. In those states, home care providers are usually required to give a copy of this list to the recipient at the first home care visit. If your state does not have such a list, you may want to consult the outline of home care clients' rights and responsibilities developed by the Commission on Legal Problems of the Elderly of the American Bar Association (reprinted in the appendix below).

APPENDIX

MODEL STATEMENT OF HOME CARE CLIENT RIGHTS AND RESPONSIBILITIES

As a home care client, you have a right to expect the following from home care providers:

1. YOU (and others whom you permit to take part in your care) SHOULD EXPECT TO BE FULLY INFORMED ABOUT YOUR SERVICES AND YOUR CHOICES BY YOUR HOME CARE AGENCY. This means that you should be informed of...

    (A) All SERVICES available from the home care agency;

    (B) CHARGES for services and whether they are covered by Medicare, Medicaid, health insurance, or other sources;

    (C) BILLING procedures, and on request, you should receive an itemized copy of each bill submitted to any payor;

    (D) the name of the home care worker and how to contact the worker's SUPERVISOR;

    (E) where and how to obtain information on the agency's licensing, certification, or accreditation standing.

2. YOU SHOULD EXPECT TO PARTICIPATE IN AND HAVE CONTROL OVER YOUR HOME CARE SER-VICES. This means that you should expect to ...

    (A) have a CHOICE in deciding who provides care services;

    (B) take an active part in creating and changing a SER-VICES PLAN, which shall be provided to you in writing in plain language. The plan must meet your approval and include the goals of care and a description of the specific tasks to be performed, by whom and when. Anyone whom you permit to participate in your care should be given an opportunity to provide input into the plan of care.

(C) have the opportunity to REFUSE all or part of any treatment, care, or service, and to be informed of the likely consequences of such refusal.

(D) receive INSTRUCTION so that you can care for yourself to the extent feasible and other participants in your care can understand your condition and effectively help.

(E) be encouraged to participate fully in COMMUNITY LIFE and exercise your civil rights, and to be assisted in doing so when assistance is needed.

(F) be asked to EVALUATE on a regular basis whether you received the care you expected to get;

(G) receive reasonable advance notice if services are to be REDUCED or TERMINATED by the provider. You should also receive help to promote a smooth transition in services appropriate for your needs.

3. YOU SHOULD EXPECT THAT YOUR RIGHTS AND PRIVILEGES AS AN ADULT IN THE COMMUNITY AND IN YOUR HOME WILL BE RESPECTED BY HOME CARE PROVIDERS. This means that the provider is a guest in your home, and you should expect...

(A) to be treated with COURTESY, RESPECT, and full recognition of your right to control your own household and lifestyle.

(B) to be assured respect and security for your home and PROPERTY.

(C) freedom from mental and physical ABUSE, NEGLECT, and exploitation.

(D) freedom from chemical and physical RESTRAINTS, except as you authorize.

(E) PRIVACY in your treatment, in caring for your personal needs, in communications, and in all daily activities.

(F) CONFIDENTIALITY of personal, financial, and medical information and records.

(G) freedom from DISCRIMINATION in the provision or quality of services based on race, religion, gender, age, or creed, or source of payment.

4. YOU SHOULD EXPECT HIGH QUALITY IN THE CARE OR SERVICES YOU RECEIVE. This means that you should...

(A) receive a PROMPT RESPONSE from the agency to your request for services, and if any request is denied, be given the reason for denial and information about what you can do.

(B) receive the services you agreed upon, EFFICIENTLY, EFFECTIVELY, and ON TIME.

(C) receive COORDINATED services when there are multiple providers or services and CONTINUITY of services when any changes are made.

(D) be served by individuals who have the TRAINING and COMPETENCE you expect.

5. YOU SHOULD EXPECT TO HAVE ANY PROBLEMS OR QUESTIONS QUICKLY ADDRESSED AND RESOLVED. This means that you should expect to...

(A) be encouraged to voice complaints and recommend changes, and be assisted in doing so when assistance is needed, WITHOUT FEAR or reprisal.

(B) receive clear instruction on HOW TO COMPLAIN to your provider and to public authorities if your care or services are not satisfactory.

(C) receive a thorough and reasonable RESPONSE to all complaints or suggestions.

CLIENT RESPONSIBILITIES

YOU (and other participants in your care) SHOULD EX-PECT TO:

1. Provide accurate and complete information relevant to your care and service plan, and any other changes in this information.

2. Take an active part in planning and managing your own care to the extent you are able.

3. Report problems to the home care agency and, if not satisfied with the response, then to public authorities.

4. Treat care and service providers with respect and dignity.

CHAPTER
9
Nursing Homes

*Types of Nursing Homes Available . . . Nursing
Home Services . . . Paying for Care . . . Evaluating
Nursing Homes . . . Admission to a Home . . .
Hospitalizations, Discharges, Transfers . . . Residents'
Rights.*

The decision that you should be placed in a nursing home
is a difficult one for both you and your family. It should be
made only after less restrictive and less costly alternatives
such as home and community-based services have been
considered. Most people enter a nursing home directly
from the hospital after a serious change in their medical
condition. Because of the severity of their illness, nursing
home care may represent the only care choice.

The selection of a nursing home is an important process,
since the nursing home often becomes the resident's home
in the final years. The degree of choice a family has depends on the amount of time available to look and to wait
before nursing home placement is necessary; on whether
the resident is placed from home or from a hospital; and on

personal finances. Unfortunately, factors beyond the control of the prospective resident frequently determine the nursing home that is selected.

Even though the choice of a nursing home may be limited by factors largely beyond your control, there are differences among facilities that you should be aware of and take into consideration.

This chapter describes the various funding sources for nursing home care; what types of care are available, depending on the source of funding; how to evaluate nursing homes; and general administrative and grievance procedures. The chapter highlights which of the provisions are applicable everywhere and which are subject to state variations. The reader is also advised to read the chapters on Medicare, Medicaid, and Supplemental Medical Insurance.

TYPES OF NURSING HOMES AVAILABLE

Are there different levels of care in nursing homes?

Yes. To understand the current situation, it helps to know a bit of recent history. Prior to October 1, 1990, federal law classified nursing homes as either skilled nursing facilities (SNFs) or health-related facilities (HRFs).

- Skilled nursing facilities provided the most intense levels of care, including around-the-clock registered nursing care; physical, speech, and occupational therapy; social services; and recreation.
- Health-related facilities provided care for persons who did not need skilled nursing care but who did need a protected environment and assistance with medication

and with activities of daily living such as walking, eating, dressing, bathing, and toileting.

Since October 1, 1990, the two-level classification system has been phased out and a single level of nursing home care has been established. Some nursing homes that were built as HRFs and do not have the structural capacity to provide SNF-level care still accept only persons who need HRF-level care; but most nursing homes now accept residents in both levels of care. Because Medicare and Medicaid reimbursement rates are generally higher for residents requiring higher levels of care, finding a nursing home placement for HRF-level residents, especially those who are confused but ambulatory and physically healthy, has become more difficult.

Who owns nursing homes?

Nursing homes may be proprietary, voluntary, or public.

- Proprietary facilities are owned and operated on a profit-making basis.
- Voluntary facilities are owned and operated on a non-profit basis, meaning that any profits from the operation of the home are put back into the facility. Voluntary facilities are usually sponsored by religious, fraternal, or community organizations.
- Public facilities are owned and operated by government agencies.

There is no way to accurately predict the quality of care that will be received solely on the basis of a facility's ownership.

What does a nursing home cost?

Nursing home rates vary tremendously from state to state and, within states, between urban and rural areas. Ask your state office for the aging or a nursing home advocacy group in your state about costs.

How can I decide which nursing homes are the most appropriate for me?

Contact your local office for the aging, your local nursing home ombudsman program, or the National Citizens Coalition for Nursing Home Reform (202-393-2018) to locate groups in your area which have information about local nursing homes. Ask social workers and other health care providers and any friends and relatives who have had experience with nursing homes. Assemble a list of nursing homes in your area to visit and use the checklist on pages 184-186 to evaluate them.

NURSING HOME SERVICES

What services must be provided by nursing homes?

All facilities must include the following services in their daily rate:
- board, including therapeutic or modified diets as prescribed by a physician
- lodging
- twenty-four-hour-per-day nursing care
- the use of all equipment and medical supplies, including but not limited to catheters, hypodermic syringes and needles, irrigation outfits, dressings, and pads

- the use of customarily stocked equipment, including but not limited to wheelchairs, crutches, and walkers
- fresh bed linen, as required, changed at least twice a week, or as often as required for incontinent residents
- hospital gowns or pajamas, unless the resident or family chooses to provide them
- laundry services for washable clothing
- general household medicine cabinet supplies, including but not limited to nonprescription medication, materials for routine skin care, oral hygiene, and care of hair
- assistance and/or supervision, when required, with activities of daily living, including but not limited to use of toilet, bathing, feeding, and walking
- the services of the nursing home staff concerned with patient care
- activities program, recreational, social, and motivational, with necessary equipment and supplies
- social services

What other services must the home provide?

The home must also agree to supply or arrange for the following services:
- dental services
- physical therapy
- occupational therapy
- speech pathology services
- audiology services

What do I need to know about the staffing of the home?

Find out whether there are physicians on the staff. If so, how many are specialists available to residents? What arrangements are made for emergency treatment if the resident's doctor is not available? Which hospitals are used if a resident needs acute care?

If you or your family member needs rehabilitation therapy, ask how often the therapist is available for treatment at the nursing home. Some special nursing homes and rehabilitation hospitals provide intensive therapy.

What medical services do nursing homes provide?

Most voluntary and public homes have on-site medical services, including the services of physicians on salary. The physicians' services are included in the basic rate. Other homes arrange for medical services to be provided on a fee-for-service basis by physicians in the community. These physicians are paid by Medicare Part B, Medicaid, private insurance, or the resident's own money.

Can I continue to use my own doctor after I am in the home?

Yes. If you wish to continue using your personal physician from the community for treatment in the nursing home, the home must give the physician the opportunity to apply for approval to practice in the facility and must promptly evaluate such a request. If the facility permits the physician to practice at the facility, the physician must agree to abide by all federal and state regulations.

You have the right to be treated by the physician of your choice. But if physicians' services are included in the basic rate, you may have to pay for your own physician in addition to the services included in the basic rate. If physicians' services are not included in the basic rate, the physician's fees may be partially covered by Medicare or by private insurance if the physician does not accept Medicaid payment.

PAYING FOR CARE

What public funding is available for nursing home payment?

Medicare covers some limited nursing home care, while Medicaid covers most nursing home costs for residents who are eligible for Medicaid.

What nursing home services does Medicare cover?

Unfortunately, Medicare covers very little long-term nursing home care. Medicare Part A covers care in a skilled nursing facility under very limited circumstances; all of the following conditions must be met:

(1) The patient has been in a hospital at least three consecutive days before going to a Medicare-certified facility.
(2) The patient requires further care for the condition that was treated in the hospital.
(3) The patient is admitted to the skilled nursing home within thirty days of the discharge from the hospital.
(4) A doctor certifies that the patient needs skilled nursing or skilled rehabilitation services on a daily basis.

Does Medicare Part B cover any services in a nursing home?

Yes. Even if your nursing home stay is not covered under Medicare Part A, physician's visits, physical therapy, and medical equipment and supplies will be partially reimbursed if you are enrolled in Medicare Part B.

Do I have to pay a deductible or co-insurance amount for Medicare-covered skilled nursing home services?

Yes. Medicare will pay the entire cost for the first twenty days. For the twenty-first through the hundredth day you must pay a co-payment. If you have private Medicare supplement insurance, the policy will cover the co-payment amounts.

Where do I apply for Medicare-covered nursing home services?

The nursing home processes your application and decides whether the home thinks that Medicare will cover your stay.

Is the nursing home's decision binding on Medicare?

No. The nursing home's opinion is not a Medicare determination.

What should I do if the nursing home tells me that Medicare will not cover my care?

You have the right to insist that the home submit your bill to Medicare.

How do I appeal a Medicare denial?

If Medicare officially denies your claim, you may appeal the decision if you think that you meet Medicare's requirements. Instructions for appealing a Medicare denial are on the back of the denial notice. Remember that Medicare does not cover services for people who need twenty-four-hour-a-day supervision because they are confused, unless they need skilled nursing services (see also chapter 5).

Does Medicaid cover nursing home services?

Yes. Medicaid pays for most nursing home care in this country. Many of the people who enter nursing homes as private pay patients eventually have to rely on Medicaid after their personal funds are exhausted.

What nursing home services are covered under Medicaid?

Medicaid covers an unlimited number of days of both skilled and intermediate care in nursing homes as long as nursing home care is medically necessary. See chapter 6 for the financial and other eligibility requirements for Medicaid.

In some states, you are not eligible for nursing home care if your income is above a certain amount. In those states, you are permitted to lower the amount of your income by transferring part of your income to a trust.

You should consult an attorney who specializes in Medicaid if your state has a Medicaid-eligibility income cap.

If I am eligible for Medicaid in my state, do I have to pay any portion of the Medicaid cost for nursing home coverage?

Yes. Except for certain deductions, you will have to contribute all of your income to the cost of your nursing home care. Medicaid will pay the rest of the cost not covered by your income.

What part of my income can I keep for myself?

You can keep a "personal needs allowance" for nonmedical needs in the nursing home, such as personal clothing or hygiene items, reading material, or special foods. It should not be used to pay for items covered in the home's basic rate (such as soap or tissues) or for items covered by Medicaid. The federal minimum allowance is $30 per month, but some states set higher amounts.

- Residents with no income receive their personal allowance from the Supplemental Security Income program.
- Residents with some income (Social Security, pension) keep their allowance from their income.

If you intend to return to your home from the nursing home, a monthly allowance can be set aside to pay rent or mortgage and other payments required to maintain your home.

Can any of my income and resources be used to support my family if I enter a nursing home on Medicaid?

Yes. A certain amount of your income and other financial resources can be turned over to your spouse who remains at home and will not have to be used for your nursing home costs. The Medicaid rule is called "prevention of spousal impoverishment." In 1995, the minimum monthly income allowance provided under federal law for a spouse is $1,230 and the maximum is $1,870.50, but these figures will increase slightly on July 1, 1995. The 1994 minimum spousal resource allowance was $14,964 and the maximum $74,820.

Does Medicare Supplement Insurance (Medigap) cover nursing home services?

Yes, but usually only if Medicare covers your nursing home stay and co-payments are required (see also chapter 7).

Does private health insurance cover nursing home care for persons who are still working or who have health insurance coverage as a retirement benefit?

A few policies cover limited amounts of nursing home care, generally for skilled care following a hospitalization. Check with your health insurance plan.

Does long-term care insurance cover nursing home services?

Yes. See the information in chapter 7.

What if I want to pay privately?

If you have income and resources over the Medicaid limits and your nursing home care does not qualify for Medicare coverage or coverage under a long-term care insurance policy, you can be admitted as a private pay resident.

Private pay rates vary from home to home and do not always include the same services. Private pay rates are not regulated and, except in Minnesota, are considerably more than the Medicare or Medicaid rates. Private pay rates can be expected to go up at least once a year, but you are entitled to thirty days' written notice before rates are raised.

EVALUATING NURSING HOMES

What questions should I ask when I visit the nursing home?

Ask for a copy of the home's admissions policy. Find out whether there is a waiting list and, if so, when a bed will be available. Also ask how long applications are kept on file, when they must be updated to be kept active, and what forms are required in your state for admission.

What should I look for when I visit a nursing home?

The physical plant:
- Is it adequately maintained, clean, well-lit, relatively odor-free?
- Is it home-like or very institutional?
- Do residents' rooms have some personal belongings, such as pictures, a plant, an afghan?
- How many beds are there in a room? Are single rooms available? Who gets them?
- Is there a policy on personal belongings and assuring they are kept safe?
- Is there an outdoor area where residents can sit, and is it being used?

The residents:
- Are they clean, dressed, and well-groomed? Is their hair combed? Are their nails trimmed?
- Are most of them out of bed?
- Are they occupied with some activity or just staring at a TV set or a blank wall?
- Are they talking with each other and the staff or are they isolated in their own private worlds?

The staff:
- Are staff neatly dressed and well-groomed?
- Do you see staff members on the floor, actually assisting residents?
- Do they speak respectfully to the residents and honor their privacy?
- Are call bells and requests for assistance answered promptly?

The food:
- Does the food look appetizing? Is it served at the proper temperature?
- Do the residents who need help with eating get this help promptly?
- Do most of the home's residents eat in the dining room?
- Does someone notice if a resident does not come to a meal or is not eating?
- Are substitutes for the main dish readily available?
- Is the menu posted and does it reflect what is actually being served?

The activities room:
- Is it well-equipped and staffed?
- Is it being used by residents?

- Is a list of activities posted?
- Are efforts made to get residents to community activities as well as to bring outsiders into the home?
- Is there a volunteer program?

One more thing to check: the most recent inspection report, which the home must make available upon request. The report lists problems found by inspectors. Read it, then find out what the home is doing to correct any listed problems.

How important is the location of the nursing home?

The nearness of a nursing home to family and friends of the resident is often a crucial factor in the adjustment of the resident to nursing home life and the quality of care received. Frequent visits from family and friends lessen the resident's feelings of isolation. Families who visit often are able to see whether the care that is given is adequate and can participate in decisions affecting the resident's care. They also can serve as advocates for the resident when problems arise.

Is a large home better than a smaller one?

Homes vary in size from under 50 to over 1,000 residents. The size of a home has a definite effect on the atmosphere. Large homes may look more "institutional" while smaller homes may be "homey." A large home will have more staff, which may make personal relationships between staff and residents more difficult to establish. Large homes, however, usually have more professionals on staff (the heads of social service, dietary, and rehabilitation departments, for example) and offer services such as dentistry and psychiatry on site, while smaller homes may rely on part-time consultants and hospital clinics for such services.

Do certain homes cater to residents of a particular religious, racial, or ethnic background?

Federal law prohibits discrimination in admission to nursing homes based on race, color, national origin, or handicap. Since nursing homes are paid for mainly through public funds (Medicaid and Medicare), the law supports the rights of individuals to gain admission to the home of their choice. In practice, some homes have residents who belong predominately to one ethnic or religious group. Some homes have a historical tradition of service to a specific ethnic or religious group. Others have tried to create an atmosphere through staff, activities, and menus that appeal to a specific culture. A resident who speaks a language other than English may feel more comfortable where other residents and staff speak the same language. Some homes try to include in their menus ethnic fare that will appeal to their resident population.

Are all residents grouped together in the home?

In some homes, residents are grouped according to the kind of care they need, their disability, or their degree of mental alertness. Alert residents often prefer to be with similarly alert people. On the other hand, confused residents often benefit from being with people who are more alert.

Will I have trouble finding a nursing home if I or my relative has Alzheimer's disease?

Recently, many homes have developed special services or units for residents with Alzheimer's disease or other dementias. Currently there are no regulations determining what services and staffing these units must have. Some facilities have the equivalent of a day care program within the home. Residents can spend much of the day in a safe and supervised environment in a less institutional setting. In the most effective programs, the staff has had special training to work with persons with dementia.

Other homes may claim to have special services, but a closer inspection may reveal nothing more than a floor where all the persons with dementia are housed without special activities or trained staff. Remember that at this time all nursing homes have a large percentage of dementia patients. A facility with a well-run activities program that caters to all the needs of its residents may provide care that is as good as the care offered by a home with a designated dementia unit.

How can I evaluate a dementia unit in a nursing home?

When evaluating a home with a special dementia unit, ask these questions:

- Is the Alzheimer's unit a separate area with skilled staff or is it simply a floor of the home where all the dementia patients are roomed?
- Has the staff received special training to work in this unit?

- Is the staff-to-resident ratio adequate to accommodate the special needs of these residents?
- Will my family member be able to take advantage of the activities offered in this unit?
- Is my family member's functional level higher or lower than that of most residents in this program?
- Will my relative be permitted to stay in the unit if my relative continually wanders?
- How does the staff handle disruptive behavior?
- If your family member is paying privately, is there an extra fee for residents of the dementia unit, and if so, what special services does it include?
- If your family member doesn't sleep well at night, how will this be addressed?
- What safety measures are utilized to protect residents who may try to leave?

How can my family member and I decide among nursing homes?

After visiting the homes on your list, you will have a basis for comparison and choice. If at all possible, have your family member visit the most promising ones and participate in making the decision. If your family member is not able to visit the home, describe what you've seen and discuss your family member's priorities. List the characteristics that are priorities for your family member (for example, location, language, availability of special services, special diet) and how well each of the homes meets these requirements. Weigh the pros and cons of each home, including the availability of a bed and the amount of time you have before placement is absolutely necessary. After you make your choices, follow up with the necessary applications.

How can I make sure that my family member receives adequate care in the nursing home?

The care your family member receives in a nursing home depends on many factors, including your involvement. There is no sure way of knowing in advance that the home you have chosen will provide even adequate care.

ADMISSION TO A HOME

What papers will I have to fill out to apply for admission to a nursing home?

The most important papers are the application form, the admission agreement, and the fee schedule. You will also be given a statement of residents' rights, medical consent forms, a resident handbook, and information about complaint procedures.

What should I look for in an admission agreement?

The admission agreement is a legal contract and can be very confusing because of the way it is written. It is a good idea to have a nursing home advocate, an ombudsman, or an attorney review the agreement before you sign it.

Can nursing homes require another person to cosign the admission agreement?

Federal law prohibits nursing homes from requiring third-party guarantees of payment as a condition of admission or of continued stay in a Medicare- or Medicaid-certified nursing home. Other legal obligations which some nursing homes may ask co-signers to assume include authorizations for medical consent, providing financial information, making funeral arrangements, or providing certain personal items. Anyone who is asked to co-sign a nursing home admission agreement should read it very carefully and should ask an advocate, ombudsman, or lawyer to review it as well.

What information does a fee schedule contain?

Before admission to a nursing home, residents or their family members receive a written notice of the services included in the home's daily rate and a written notice of services not included in the daily rate for which the resident may be charged and the charges for those services. This information may be in the admission agreement or in a separate fee schedule.

Do nursing homes require down payments or deposits?

Yes. If you or your family member is not on Medicaid, homes require advance payments. Some states limit the amount of advance payment allowed to three months.

Can a nursing home require a resident or the resident's family to pay privately for a certain period of time?

No. Duration-of-stay requirements are illegal under federal law. Many private pay residents eventually use up their savings and become eligible for Medicaid.

Can a nursing home demand or accept donations from family members to ensure admission to the home?

No. This practice is also illegal under federal law. Any solicitations of this kind should be reported to the Attorney General's office or the Medicaid fraud unit in your state.

Will it be more difficult for me to be admitted to a nursing home if I am on Medicaid before I apply?

Unfortunately, yes. Federal law requires Medicare- and Medicaid-certified facilities to use the same rules regarding transfer, discharge, and provision of service for all residents regardless of source of payment, but does not obligate nursing homes to accept all Medicaid recipients who apply to them. Because the private pay rates are higher, most homes admit private pay patients in preference to Medicaid patients. States contract with nursing homes that participate in the Medicaid program and often allow them to designate a certain number of beds for Medicaid patients. These homes may reserve their Medicaid beds for private pay patients who become eligible for Medicaid after using up their funds rather than admitting Medicaid-eligible patients from outside the home.

If I apply as a private pay patient, what financial information will the home request?

Most homes require full financial disclosure from private pay patients to determine how long the resident will be able to pay privately before going on Medicaid.

What is a comprehensive care plan meeting?

Within the first two weeks after a resident enters a facility, staff representing all disciplines meet with the resident and/or family to create a plan of care. This is a very important meeting for you and your family members to attend so that you can understand exactly what care you can expect. It is a time to ask questions, to give information about your habits and history, and to explain your likes and dislikes. Patients and families are invited to this meeting at least once a year, but the staff reviews the plan quarterly or when there is a significant change in the resident's condition. In addition, patients and families can arrange for a meeting whenever they have a concern that needs the attention of the care team.

HOSPITALIZATIONS, DISCHARGES, TRANSFERS

Will the nursing home keep my bed available if I have to go to a hospital?

When you leave your nursing home temporarily — to be hospitalized or to visit a family member or for another reason — federal law protects your right to be readmitted to the home. You are entitled to the first available semi-private room, as long as you require the same care which you required previously.

Will I or my family have to pay the full cost of the bed while I am away?

That depends upon how you are paying for the nursing home.

- If you are paying privately, you will have to pay yourself to maintain your bed.
- The number of days that Medicaid will pay for a bed hold and whether Medicaid will pay during a home visit varies from state to state. In some states, Medicaid will pay the nursing home to hold the resident's bed; however, in some states, Medicaid does not pay for any bed hold days and the resident's family or friends must pay at the private pay rate to reserve the bed.
- Medicare does not pay to keep a bed open while a nursing home patient is in the hospital.

If you or your relative is not on Medicaid, be sure to find out the home's bed reservation policy.

What notice is the nursing home required to give me about its bed reservation policies?

Federal law requires that notice be given by the home in writing to any resident who is being transferred for hospitalization or leave of the state Medicaid bed-hold period and the policy of the home. This notice must also be given to a member of the resident's family or to the resident's legal representative.

When can residents be discharged or transferred?

Residents may be discharged or transferred to another facility only when the interdisciplinary care team determines that:

(1) the transfer or discharge is necessary for the resident's welfare and the resident's needs cannot be met at the facility;

(2) the resident's health has improved sufficiently so the resident no longer needs the services provided by the facility;

(3) the health or safety of others at the facility is endangered; or

(4) the resident has failed, after reasonable notice, to pay an allowable charge imposed by the facility for an item or service requested by the resident and for which the resident may be charged above the basic rate.

The facility must include the resident and designated representative in formulating a discharge plan that will meet the needs of the resident.

What notice must the home give a resident before a transfer or discharge?

Any time a facility wishes to discharge or transfer a resident, the resident and designated representative must receive a written notice that explains the reasons for the transfer and how to appeal. This notice must be given at least thirty days in advance, unless

- the safety or the health of the individuals in the home is endangered;

- the resident no longer needs the services of the home, and the resident's health has improved sufficiently to allow a more immediate discharge;

- a more immediate transfer or discharge is necessitated by the resident's urgent medical needs; or

- the resident has not resided in the home for more than thirty days.

What appeal rights do I have if I disagree with a transfer or discharge planned by the home?

Federal law requires that states provide a fair hearing process to appeal transfers and discharges initiated by the home. Check with your state nursing home ombudsman program to find out how to appeal in your state. These programs are listed in chapter 11.

Can the home transfer me to another floor or bed without my consent?

Federal law requires that notice be given before your room or your roommate is changed by the facility, but does not expressly provide a time period or appeal rights for these changes.

RESIDENTS' RIGHTS

What rights are guaranteed to nursing home residents?

People who live in nursing homes have the same personal rights as people who live in the community. Sometimes nursing homes abuse these rights in the interest of institutional efficiency. Nursing home staff, and even family members, sometimes need to be reminded that many nursing home residents are fully capable of making decisions for themselves, have the right to do so, and should be encouraged to do so.

Certain rights are guaranteed by federal law, and many states also have their own versions of these rights guaranteed under state law. The home must train its staff to honor residents' rights and inform each newly admitted resident and the resident's family about the resident's rights and responsibilities. In addition, a summary of this information must be posted in a prominent place in the facility.

What specific rights does federal law guarantee to nursing home residents?

The following is a list of nursing home residents' rights:

- The right to be encouraged and assisted to exercise one's rights as a citizen to voice grievances, pursue legal remedies, and recommend changes in policy and services to facility staff and/or outside representatives of one's choice, free from restraint, interference, coercion, discrimination, or reprisal
- The right to participate in the facility's residents' council
- The right to communicate privately with persons of one's choice
- The right to send and receive one's personal mail unopened
- The right to join with other residents or persons within or outside the facility for improvements in patient care
- The right to meet with social, religious, and community groups and to participate in their activities
- The right to privacy for visits by one's spouse, partner, or relative and to share a room with one's partner or relative if both are residents of the facility
- The right to exercise one's civil and religious liberties
- The right to make independent personal decisions and to be informed about available choices

Can the home require that I deposit my personal allowance with them?

No. The home must have a system for keeping an account of each resident's personal allowance but may not require residents to deposit their funds with the facility. The resident may give the allowance to a friend or relative each month, open a bank account, or instruct the nursing home to give the allowance to the same person each month.

If the resident chooses to use the home's service, the home must keep a separate accounting of the resident's funds. The home must also keep funds over $50 in an interest-bearing account and must give the resident or the resident's legal representative reasonable access to the account records. In addition, some states require that a monthly or quarterly statement be given to the resident. If the resident is on Medicaid, the home must notify the resident when the amount in the resident's account reaches $200 less than the resource limit for Medicaid or for SSI.

If the resident becomes too confused to use the personal allowance, the family should arrange with the home to use the allowance for the benefit of the resident. Many homes will reimburse family members with the funds from the resident's personal allowance when they present receipts for clothing or other items for the resident's use.

If a family member is willing to handle all the resident's finances, he can apply to the Social Security Administration to become the resident's representative payee and receive the resident's Social Security check on his behalf.

Each month this family member will deposit the check and write a check to the nursing home for the amount of the resident's income less the personal allowance.

When the resident dies, the home must give a final statement of the account to the next of kin. Any balance in the account goes to the resident's estate and can be used to help pay for burial expenses.

What if I cannot exercise my rights as a nursing home resident?

If you are unable to exercise rights because of a determination of legal incapacity or have been found by a physician to be mentally incapable of understanding them, or cannot communicate, you can exercise your rights if you have a "designated representative." Generally, a guardian or a health care agent is your designated representative, but state laws vary on this issue. The role of your designated representative should be documented in your records. Your designated representative should receive any required written or oral information and should be involved with your treatment plan.

What rights does a resident have regarding visits?

Residents have the right to know the home's visiting hours. They have the right to visit with family members at any time and with others at reasonable hours of the day or evening. Outsiders have no legal right to visit nursing home residents. Rather, it is each resident's right to receive visitors. Thus, anyone with whom a resident wishes to visit has the right to enter the nursing home. Anyone whom a resident does not wish to see does not have this right.

What rights do I have regarding my personal possessions?

Federal regulations provide that residents have the right to keep and use personal belongings except where the health or safety of the individual or other residents would be endangered. You should negotiate with the home if you disagree with the home's interpretation of this rule.

Do I have the right to refuse restraints?

All competent nursing home residents have the right to refuse treatment after being informed of the risks of doing so. This applies to the use of physical and chemical restraints as well.

Since 1990, federal law has required that restraints be avoided whenever possible and used only to ensure physical safety. They must be prescribed by a physician and the order must specify how long and under what circumstances the restraints may be used.

What are physical restraints?

Physical restraints are devices or appliances that are used to restrict movement. If too tightly applied, they can cause brush burns, bruises, blisters, and poor circulation. If they are too loosely applied, the patient may slip through or become entangled in them. Improper use results in muscular atrophy and increases the risk of upper respiratory, urinary tract, and skin problems. Besides being dangerous, physical restraints also undermine a person's dignity and independence.

How can physical restraints be avoided?

Other measures — such as changing the position of a pillow, using a footrest, or finding a chair better suited to the resident's body size — should be tried before physical restraints are used. Nursing homes that have tried these alternatives have been able to reduce the use of restraints significantly.

What are chemical restraints?

Chemical restraints are drugs given primarily for controlling a resident's behavior. Chemical restraints, such as haldol, thorazine, and mellaril, should be used only for psychiatric symptoms, such as hallucinations or delusions, and not to control the behavior of residents. Use of these medications to deal with difficult behavior can be a way for the home to avoid examining the causes of the behavior. Agitated behavior often results from fear, boredom, thirst, or hunger. When staff members address these underlying problems, it is often possible to reduce the use of these drugs.

What problems can chemical restraints cause?

Chemical restraints often cause drowsiness and disorientation. Long-term use may cause a neurological disorder called tardive dyskinesia, manifested by twitching of the hands, arms, and legs and involuntary movements of the mouth and facial muscles. These drugs can have other serious side effects, such as incontinence and pneumonia.

What can I do if I am dissatisfied with the nursing home?

Try to resolve the problem with the nursing home staff. If this does not work, turn to the formal grievance procedures of the nursing home (most homes have internal grievance procedures) or consider these alternatives:

- Work with the residents' council and the family council (many nursing homes have residents' councils which deal with issues and complaints within a home, and some homes also have family member councils which can also be of assistance in resolving issues).
- Contact the state long-term care ombudsman. Every state is required, under the Older Americans Act, to have such an ombudsman program. Ombudsmen must investigate and try to resolve complaints made by nursing home residents. A list of state ombudsman programs can be found in chapter 11.
- Contact a local nursing home advocacy group. You can locate these through your residents' council or through the National Citizens Coalition for Nursing Home Reform in Washington, D.C., 202-393-2018.

CHAPTER

10

Creating a
Lifetime Plan

*Lifetime Planning . . . Surrogate Financial
Management . . . Surrogate Decision Making for
Health Care . . . Court-Appointed Guardianship.*

Today's Americans are living longer than those of even one generation ago, and most can look forward to a vigorous life well into their eighties or nineties. Although most people remain fully capable of managing their own affairs in old age, there is an increasing possibility that people reaching very advanced old age will need help with the tasks of daily living from family members, friends, or professionals. Tasks of daily living consist of paying bills, submitting medical claims to insurance companies, applying for public benefits, balancing checkbooks, making sure that the home is safe and comfortable, obtaining home care workers, and making doctor's appointments. Family members and friends may eventually also be asked to help make important health care decisions when the patient cannot give consent for treatment.

The potential for increased dependency in advanced old age has recently led elderly persons and their families to seek new approaches to planning for a secure old age. One such approach is called "lifetime planning," a variation of the traditional practice of estate planning. Lifetime planning includes giving a trusted relative or friend the legal authority to act on your behalf in case your ability to manage your financial or personal affairs has been diminished or lost. Lifetime planning requires that you give them instructions on your particular lifestyle wishes, values, and obligations so that they can step into your shoes and make decisions that are similar to those you would have made yourself, if you were capable of doing so. Appointing another person to take care of your affairs, before he or she is needed, will give you the assurance that your wishes will be honored and that your appointed agent will be prepared to take on the role of caregiver according to your instructions.

The most dramatic case for lifetime planning is made in its absence — when someone falls seriously ill or becomes mentally impaired without having given another person the authority to take responsibility for his or her financial and personal affairs. All too often, loved ones are then faced with a crisis. They are thrown into the role of caregiver without having the legal authority to deposit or withdraw funds from bank accounts, pay bills, or to make decisions about needed medical care for which "informed consent" is required. Without such authority, they may have to go to court to obtain guardianship so that they can be given the needed legal authority through a court order. This legal process is often painful, costly, and time-consuming. Furthermore, court-ordered guardianship does not ensure that the person of choice is appointed guardian over financial or personal affairs, nor is it likely that such a court-appointed guardian will make decisions identical to the decisions the patient would have made.

However difficult it is for you to consider the possibility that someone else may some day need to manage your affairs, planning for that eventuality is a central feature of lifetime planning. Since each state has its own laws concerning delegation of financial or health care decision making, it is advisable to contact an attorney in your state who is familiar with elder law and who knows the particular options available under your state's laws.

This chapter considers how you can plan ahead and voluntarily delegate authority over your financial affairs; how you can appoint someone to make health care decisions for you; and finally what will happen if you don't plan ahead and someone has to go to court to request that a guardian be appointed with the authority to manage your financial or personal affairs.

LIFETIME PLANNING

What is the difference between estate planning and lifetime planning?

Estate planning is concerned with planning for the security of your dependents and the disposition of your estate according to your wishes after your death.

Lifetime planning, on the other hand, is focused on advanced old age and a period of your life when chronic medical conditions, physical frailty, and mental impairment may require the involvement of another person to maintain your lifestyle and assist you with the activities of daily living. Lifetime planning is a process in which you consider such questions as:

- Who should be authorized to have access to my bank accounts or other financial arrangements if I cannot take care of my affairs myself?
- Who should be given authority to make health care decisions on my behalf, if I do not have the ability to make those critical decisions?
- At what point in my life should authorized people take over control over financial or health care decisions?

When should I make a lifetime plan?

Ideally all people, old or young, should make lifetime plans while they are healthy and do not need another person to make decisions for them. For older people of advanced age, who run a greater risk of needing someone in the future who can make critical financial and health care decisions, it is particularly important. The objective of lifetime planning is to maintain control over your life and prepare for the "worst case scenario," such as becoming impaired because of Alzheimer's disease. Having a lifetime plan is a type of insurance against the possible catastrophe of losing control over your life and having no one ready and available to step into your shoes.

If I have a will, do I still need to make a lifetime plan?

Yes. A lifetime plan will consider such issues as who will be responsible for your affairs during your lifetime, in the event that you cannot take care of your finances or other personal decisions. A will, on the other hand, deals with your estate after your death. It is usually a good idea to have both.

Surrogate Financial Management

What are the options available for surrogate financial management?

There are several common legal arrangements that you can initiate to have someone else manage your finances at some point in the future:

• Durable power of attorney
• Springing power of attorney
• Revocable living trust
• Irrevocable living trust
• Joint ownership

What is a power of attorney?

A power of attorney is essentially a contract between you and another person of your choice by which you give the other person the legal authority to gain access to your financial affairs. When you create a power of attorney, you are the "principal" and the person appointed by you to carry out your wishes is the "agent." A power of attorney can be very broad and cover all possible financial accounts and transactions, or it can be very narrow and allow your agent to manage only your checking account for everyday money management.

When should I create a power of attorney?

Powers of attorney can only be created when you, the principal, have the mental ability to know what the creation of this contract means, and you are acting at your own free will. A regular power of attorney usually is valid only while you have the mental capacity to direct your agent and supervise his or her actions. It becomes useless after you have lost the ability to oversee the actions of your agent. In order to overcome this serious disadvantage, there are other types of powers of attorney that address this concern. They are durable powers of attorney and springing durable powers of attorney.

What is a durable power of attorney?

A durable power of attorney is similar to a regular power of attorney with one major difference: the durable power of attorney remains valid even if you no longer can direct your agent and supervise his or her actions. A durable power of attorney usually indicates that the power of attorney will remain valid despite the incompetency or incapacity of the principal. If you are planning for the possibility of your own mental incapacity, a durable power of attorney is therefore much more useful than a regular power of attorney, since the agent can continue to take care of your affairs after you can no longer do so yourself, exactly when you need him or her most.

What is a springing durable power of attorney?

A springing power of attorney is similar to a durable power of attorney, except for the fact that a springing power of attorney does not go into effect right away. Instead, it goes into effect at some future time or at some future event that you have determined ahead of time. (It is called a "springing" power of attorney because it "springs" into effect at the time you have determined that it should.) This means that you could appoint your agent today but delay giving him or her access to your affairs until some time later. Under a springing power of attorney you would be planning for a future event, instruct and appoint your agent accordingly, and your agent would only act in your stead if and when that triggering event has taken place.

Does every state have these types of powers of attorney?

Powers of attorney are generally available in most states; however, each state has its own laws that prescribe the details. If you wish to create a regular, durable, or springing power of attorney, you should contact a local attorney for specific options in your state.

Who can create a power of attorney?

Any adult of sound mind can create a power of attorney to manage his or her financial affairs. No other person can create a power of attorney for you. Thus, if you never had given a power of attorney and you became unable to manage your finances because of a serious illness that affected your mental powers, the option would be unavailable.

Who should be my agent?

Since an agent manages your funds, it is important that you fully trust him or her. An agent could be a family member or a friend who is willing and able to take on the considerable responsibility of managing your affairs. It is usually advantageous to appoint someone who lives close to you so that he or she will know when you need help.

Can I appoint more than one agent to have power of attorney?

Yes, in most states you can appoint more than one person to have power of attorney over your financial affairs. If you want to have two or more agents, you may decide whether you want them to act jointly (by requiring that the signatures of both are needed at all times) or to be able to act separately.

What are the benefits of a power of attorney?

The benefits of a power of attorney are that you have chosen the person who will act in your stead and have instructed him or her to make decisions just as you would have made them yourself, if you were still capable of making financial decisions. By having a legally authorized agent you can rest assured that your affairs will be taken care of, that bills will be paid, and that your general lifestyle will not be affected too much by your inability to manage your own financial affairs.

What are the disadvantages of powers of attorney?

A serious disadvantage is that you cannot entirely eliminate the possibility of being harmed by an untrustworthy agent. Powers of attorney can be quite easily created, but there is no organization or other entity that monitors the actions of agents. There is evidence that some agents abuse the powers of attorney given them for their own benefit. It is for this reason that it is also advisable to appoint two people who can monitor each other's actions.

What is a trust?

A trust is a legal instrument by which someone (often called the "grantor") transfers property to another (the "trustee"), who is obligated by law and by the trust agreement to manage the property for the benefit of someone (the "beneficiary"). Each trust agreement is tailored to the individual circumstances of the grantor and the beneficiaries. There are no standard forms, and specific details of the trust need to be worked out by the grantor in consultation with an attorney.

How can a trust help me with a lifetime plan?

Trusts have long been used to convey gifts or inheritances. But they have another use as well. You can create a trust by which another person will be able to manage your financial affairs in the event you can no longer do so yourself.

The kind of trust involved is a trust for your own benefit, not merely for the benefit of dependents or survivors. You are the beneficiary of this kind of trust during your lifetime. The term "living trust" is sometimes used to describe it.

Who will manage my trust?

When you transfer your property into any trust, the funds will be managed by the trustee that you select. The trustee receives very specific instructions through the trust agreement about how you want the property managed for the beneficiaries.

You can, if you choose, name yourself as the trustee of your living trust. If you do that, you can manage the trust while you have the capacity to manage your affairs. But to achieve the goals of lifetime planning, you would also appoint another person to take over from you as successor trustee if and when you lose the capacity to manage your affairs. (The successor trustee can also take over after your death, to manage the trust for your chosen beneficiaries.)

What is a revocable living trust?

A revocable trust is a trust agreement that can be rewritten and changed by you during your lifetime whenever you change your mind.

What is an irrevocable living trust?

An irrevocable trust is a trust agreement which cannot be changed after it has been created. There may be some tax advantages to an irrevocable living trust.

Does the existence of a trust affect eligibility for public benefits?

It may. In some instances, the existence of a trust may disqualify the *grantor* (the one who created the trust) when he or she later applies for Medicaid or some other public benefit. Similarly, being the *beneficiary* of a trust may make one ineligible for some public benefits. In recent years, Medicaid law has been revised to restrict the use of trusts for lifetime planning and estate planning purposes. As a consequence, if you plan to create a trust for yourself or your dependents, you should always consult an attorney who is thoroughly familiar with public benefit law.

What is meant by joint ownership of an account?

Joint ownership of bank accounts enables you to give another person of your choice access to your bank account.
Joint ownership can be created in one of three ways, depending on whether you wish to have the joint owner be
able to act on his or her own, or to act together with
you, or to gain access only after your death. Below are
examples of joint bank accounts in the names of John
Doe and Mary Smith:

- "John Doe *or* Mary Smith." This account would enable John and Mary each to act alone. It would be useful for John's lifetime plan, since Mary would always
be able to use it on behalf of John if John loses the
ability to manage his affairs. In addition, if John dies,
Mary would have full ownership of the account. The
risk with this type of account is that Mary as well as
John will be considered owners of the account, even
though only John's money was used to set it up. That
can be a serious disadvantage for Mary if she needs to
apply for a public benefit, because the funds in the account will be considered an asset of Mary's.

- "John Doe *and* Mary Smith." This account would require the signatures of both John and Mary for any
transaction; the problem with this type of account is
that when one of the owners becomes incapacitated
the account can no longer be accessed by the other
owner. Thus it is not wise to set up an account in this
form for purposes of lifetime planning.

- "John Doe *in trust for* Mary Smith." This account will
be available to Mary only after John's death. An "in
trust for" account is sometimes used to act like a will

in situations where there are very limited assets or if John wants Mary to have access to the funds immediately after his death (for instance to pay for his funeral).

- "Mary Smith *in trust for* John Doe." This type of account is useful for lifetime planning since it allows Mary to use the account for John during his lifetime when he cannot manage his own affairs. In addition, this type of account will not be considered an asset of Mary's and thus will not disqualify her from becoming eligible for public benefits since the account can only be considered an asset of John's. Where a significant amount of money is involved, it is always best to consult an attorney before setting up a joint account.

What are the disadvantages of joint ownership?

Like a power of attorney, it is the type of arrangement which requires that you fully trust the person you name on the account.

Furthermore, a serious disadvantage is that joint ownership of an account may negatively affect the ability of one of the owners to gain access to a public benefit that has income and resource limitations. Many "needs-based" public benefits, such as Medicaid, consider a joint bank account to be 100 percent available to the applicant of the benefit. As a result, the applicant may be denied benefits, because it is assumed that the applicant has more money in the bank than is allowed. Thus, for people who need to apply for Medicaid or Supplemental Security Income, a joint bank account may not be an advantage.

SURROGATE DECISION MAKING FOR HEALTH CARE

What are "advance directives"?

"Advance directive" is a general term that applies to two kinds of legal documents:

- the living will (sometimes called a "directive to physicians," "health care declaration," or "medical directive")
- the durable power of attorney for health care (sometimes called a "health care proxy")

The purpose of these documents is to enable you to give instructions about your future medical care, in the event that you become unable to speak for yourself due to serious illness or incapacity. Each state regulates the use of advance directives differently.

Why do I need an advance directive?

Advance directives give you a voice in decisions about your medical care, even when you are unconscious or too ill to communicate. As long as you are able to make decisions and express them, you can accept or refuse any medical treatment. But if you become seriously ill, you may lose the ability to participate in decisions about your own treatment. Having a living will or a health care agent will help your loved ones to decide for you without too much anguish.

What is a living will?

A living will is a written expression of your wishes about medical treatment should you be at the end of your life and unable to communicate. Its purpose is to guide your family and doctors in deciding how aggressively to use medical treatments to delay your dying.

Your state law may define when the living will goes into effect, and it may limit the treatments to which the living will applies. Also, the state law generally supplies a standard form of living will that you may use. You should read your state's standard document carefully to be sure that it reflects your wishes. If it doesn't, you can add further instructions or write your own living will to cover situations that the state document may not address.

Keep in mind that your right to accept or to refuse treatment is protected by constitutional and common law. Thus, even if your state does not have a "living will law," it is wise to put your wishes about the use of life-sustaining treatments in writing.

What is a durable power of attorney for health care?

A durable power of attorney for health care is a document that lets you appoint someone you trust to make decisions about your medical care if you cannot make those decisions yourself. This type of advance directive may also be called a "health care proxy" or "appointment of a health care agent." The person you appoint may be called your health care agent, surrogate, attorney-in-fact, or proxy.

The person you appoint through a durable power of attorney for health care is authorized to deal with all medical situations when you cannot speak for yourself, not only end-of-life decisions. Thus, he or she can speak for you if you become temporarily incapacitated — after an accident, for example — as well as when you become irreversibly ill.

Generally, the law requires your agent to make the same medical decisions that you would have made, if you had been able to voice your opinion. To do this, your agent should examine any specific statements you have made, your religious and moral beliefs, and your values in general. The intent of a health care power of attorney is that your agent will stand in your shoes and speak with your voice. If your wishes about a particular medical decision are not known, your agent must act in your best interest, using his or her own judgment.

Some states let you appoint an agent within the living will form. This is different from a durable power of attorney for health care, because an agent appointed in a living will can make decisions only about using life-support treatments, and only if you are in one of the medical conditions (such as "terminally ill," "permanently unconscious," or "imminently dying") specified in the state's living will law.

Why bother with an advance directive if I want my family to make any decisions that have to be made for me?

Depending on your state's laws, your family may not be allowed to make decisions about life support for you without written evidence of your wishes. Although doctors usually turn to the next of kin to make most decisions when patients can't speak for themselves, a decision to withhold or stop life support is often handled differently because of its final nature. Some state laws do permit family members to make all medical decisions for their incapacitated loved ones. But other states require clear evidence of the patient's own wishes.

Even in states that do permit family decision making, you should still prepare advance directives for two reasons:

- You can name the person you are most comfortable with to act as your decision maker (who may or may not be your next of kin).
- Your advance directives will make your wishes known. Without knowledge of your wishes, your loved ones may be reluctant to make any decision.

Should I prepare a living will and also appoint an agent?

Yes. You can best protect your treatment wishes by having both a living will and a health care agent, because each offers something the other does not.

What are the advantages of having a health care agent?

Medical decision making is rarely simple. Treatment decisions have to be made in response to changing medical conditions, and medical situations often unfold unpredictably. Decision making involves weighing benefits and drawbacks, and even evaluating the odds for success or failure.

The person you appoint as agent can respond flexibly to changes or unanticipated situations in a way that no document can. In addition, you are legally authorizing that person to make decisions based not only on what you expressed in writing or verbally, but on knowledge of you as a person as well. Your agent can take into account other concerns you may have, such as the effect of your illness on your family, the quality of life that matters to you, and even any concerns you may have about finances.

Living wills address end-of-life decisions only. An agent appointed through a durable power of attorney for health care usually can make health care decisions in a wider range of situations than those involving end-of-life care.

What are the benefits of having a living will?

If your agent has to decide whether medical treatment should be withheld or withdrawn to permit you to die, your living will can reassure your agent that he or she is following your wishes in these most difficult decisions. In addition, if the person you appointed as agent is unavailable or unwilling to speak for you, of if other people challenge the decision not to use life-sustaining treatment, your living will can guide and direct your caregivers.

Thoughtfully prepared, a living will can be a valuable support to appointing an agent; similarly, your agent can ensure that the spirit and not just the letter of your living will is followed.

Who can serve as my agent?

Your agent can be almost any adult whom you trust to make health care decisions for you. It can be a close family member or a good friend who is willing to assume that responsibility on your behalf.

The important thing when appointing an agent is to make sure he or she understands your wishes about the use of medical treatment and is willing to respect them and to be assertive if necessary. Not everyone is comfortable making these kinds of decisions, and your agent may have to be persistent in order to have your wishes respected. Therefore, it is essential that you talk to the person before appointing him or her, even if it is your spouse, adult child, or other family member.

Is there anyone who cannot serve as my agent?

Under most state laws, you cannot appoint your attending physician as your agent, and in some states your agent cannot be any health care worker caring for you in a medical facility.

Can I appoint more than one agent?

You should not (and in many states you may not) appoint more than one person to act at the same time, because it can cause conflicts and confusion. The result may be that no decision is reached.

You can, however, appoint one or more alternate agents. If the first person you named is unwilling or unable to serve — for example, if he is ill — then the next one is called upon to act as your alternate agent, and so on down the list of alternates.

What should I tell my agent?

Your agent needs to know when and how aggressively you would want medical treatment applied.

For example, if you had a massive stroke, would you want to receive aggressive treatments (such as mechanical ventilation, antibiotics, tube feeding), for a time, but have them stopped if there were no improvement? What kind of treatment would you want if you were in a permanent coma or persistent vegetative state: a ventilator? tube feeding? comfort care only? What are your views on artificial nutrition (tube feeding)? Do you want to receive it no matter what your medical condition? On a trial basis? Never? If your heart stopped, under what circumstances would you want doctors to try to resuscitate you (using CPR)?

Talking to your agent means discussing values and quality of life issues, as well as treatments and medical situations. Since there may be situations that you did not anticipate, your agent may need to base a decision on what he or she knows about your values and your views of what makes life worth living. These are not simple questions, and your views may change. For this reason, you need to talk to your agent in depth and over time.

What if I do not have anyone to appoint as my agent?

If you have no one to appoint as your agent, it is especially important that you complete a clear living will. Be sure that your loved ones, your doctor, and anyone else who may be involved with your health care have copies of the completed document and understand your wishes about medical treatments when you are at the end of life. If you are admitted to a hospital or long-term care facility, you should have the living will made a part of your medical record.

When do my advance directives become legally valid?

Your advance directives become legally valid as soon as you sign them in front of the required witnesses. However, your advance directives will not be used as long as you are able to make your own decisions about your medical care. Each state sets its own guidelines for when advance directives become operative. The rules may differ for living wills and medical durable powers of attorney.

When does a durable power of attorney for health care go into effect?

Durable powers of attorney for health care are used only when your physician has concluded that you are unable to make your own medical decisions. Many states have an additional requirement that applies only to decisions about life support. Before your agent can refuse life-sustaining treatment on your behalf, a second physician must confirm your doctor's assessment that you are incapable of making treatment decisions.

When does a living will go into effect?

In most states, before your living will can be acted on, two physicians must certify that you are unable to make medical decisions *and* that you are in the medical condition specified in the state's living will law (such as "terminal illness" or "permanent unconsciousness").

Will my advance directives be honored in another state?

The answer varies from state to state. Some states honor advance directives from another state; others honor out-of-state documents to the extent they conform to the state's own law; and some states do not address the issue. At bottom, you have constitutional and common-law rights to accept or refuse treatment that may be even broader than your rights under any state law. A state would probably have to honor an advance directive that clearly expresses your treatment wishes.

If you reside in, or receive medical care in, more than one state, you should complete the advance directives for all of the states involved. It will be easier to have your advance directives honored if they are the ones that the medical facility is familiar with.

Do I need a lawyer to prepare advance directives?

No. You can get state-specific forms, at no charge, from Choice In Dying, Inc., an organization in New York (see below). Your local hospital, the local bar association, or the state office on aging may provide them as well. The forms come with instructions on how to complete them. Read all of the instructions carefully to be sure that your document is witnessed properly and that you have included all of the necessary information. It might be wise to ask someone else to look over the forms for you, to be sure that you have filled them out correctly.

Must my advance directives be witnessed?

Yes, every state has some witnessing requirement. Most require two adult witnesses; some also require a notary. The purpose of witnessing is to confirm that you are really the person who signed the document, that you were not forced to sign it, and that you appeared to understand what you were doing.

Who can be a witness?

All states require that your witnesses be adults. Beyond that, the requirements vary from state to state. Generally, a person you appoint as your agent or alternate agent cannot be a witness. In some states your witnesses cannot be any relative by blood or marriage or anyone who would benefit from your estate. Some states prohibit your doctor and employees of a health care institution in which you are a patient from acting as witnesses.

What should I do with my completed advance directives?

Make several photocopies of the completed forms. Keep the original forms in a safe but easily accessible place, and tell others where you put them; you can also note on the photocopies the location where the original forms are kept. Do not keep your advance directives in a safe deposit box; other people may need access to them.

Give photocopies to your agent (and alternate agent), your doctor, and everyone else who might be involved with your health care, such as your family, clergy, or friends. When you are admitted to a hospital, ask that your living will or health care power of attorney be placed in your medical file.

How can I be sure my advance directives will be honored?

Simply completing advance directives will not ensure that your wishes will be honored. These documents are tools to help the decision-making process. Their effectiveness depends largely on the way you prepare your loved ones and other caregivers for their use. Don't assume that they know what you would want; research shows that family's and physicians' guesses about a patient's preferences are often mistaken. Talking with the people who may have to act on your behalf ensures that they understand your wishes, gives them a chance to ask questions, and also lets you determine whether they will follow your wishes, even if your choices differ from theirs. To best protect your treatment wishes, you should do two things:

- Take the time to think your feelings through and express them fully, so that your advance directives truly reflect your treatment wishes.
- Talk openly about your wishes with your family, your friends, and your doctor.

Where can I get more information on advance directives?

The foremost source for information on advance directives is a national organization called Choice in Dying, Inc., located in New York City. The organization will send you free living wills and powers of attorney that are legally valid in your particular state, and it will provide you with instructions on how to fill them out. It is also available to answer questions. Choice in Dying also offers an optional service, the Living Will Registry, which includes review of your advance directives to ensure their validity and computerized filing so your documents will be available in case of a medical crisis. Choice in Dying can be called at 1-800-989-WILL.

COURT-APPOINTED GUARDIANSHIP

What may happen if I don't plan ahead?

If you do not give someone the legal authority to handle your financial affairs and you become unable to manage them yourself, someone else may have to be appointed, possibly against your wishes, to manage your income or other financial affairs for you. There are basically two types of "surrogates" or "fiduciaries" that could be appointed to handle financial matters:

• Guardians

• Representative payees (discussed in chapter 1)

What is a guardian?

A guardian, also called a conservator in some states, is a person appointed by a court of law, after a full court proceeding, to manage your financial or personal affairs because the court has found that you can no longer adequately manage your affairs yourself.

How does the guardianship process begin?

It usually starts with a petition, submitted to the court by someone (a family member, a friend, a health care facility, or the county social services agency) to request that the court appoint a guardian over your financial affairs.

Will I know ahead of time that a petition has been made in my case?

Yes. The courts are obligated to notify you immediately after a petition has been filed. The notice will explain why the petition has been made, inform you of your right to be present or to be represented at the hearing, and tell you when the court hearing will take place.

If I don't agree that a guardianship is necessary, can I obtain a lawyer to represent me in court?

Yes. You have the right to be represented by a lawyer of your own choice. Furthermore, if you cannot afford a lawyer, you can ask the judge to assign one to represent you. You also have the right to bring witnesses to your hearing to refute the statements made by the petitioner in your case.

How does the judge decide whether a guardian is needed?

You have the right to be present at the hearing so that the judge can listen to you and your witnesses and balance your evidence against the evidence that will be presented by the petitioner. At the hearing, testimony from doctors and other experts is sometimes required to verify to the judge that your mental capacity is so diminished that you lack the ability to make informed decisions. The judge may also appoint a "guardian ad litem" to interview you and to determine whether the petitioner is correct. A guardian ad litem does not represent you; he or she is a fact finder for the court and makes recommendations to the judge.

If a guardian is appointed, does he or she manage all my affairs?

In general, the courts are obligated to order the least restrictive guardianship that can meet your needs. In some states, the judge can appoint a limited or a temporary guardian. However, judges have the power to give the guardian very broad authority over your affairs if they deem that necessary. A guardian can be appointed not only to manage your financial affairs, but also to make health care decisions for you, if needed.

Who is usually appointed as guardian?

Court-appointed guardians can be family members or friends, but the decision as to who will be appointed is ultimately up to the judge who presides over your case. In some cases, the judge might even appoint a bank, an attorney, or the county social service agency to act as your guardian.

What happens when a guardian has been appointed?

Once a guardian has been appointed, you lose control over your own affairs to the extent of the guardian's authority. If the guardian has general control over your finances, the guardian makes decisions about how to pay your bills, how to invest your money, or whether or not to sell your assets.

Why can't a representative payee do what a guardian does?

As explained in chapter 1, a representative payee is a person appointed by the Social Security Administration to receive your Social Security or supplemental security income check for you. A representative payee's authority is limited. He or she is legally authorized to manage only your Social Security or Supplemental Security Income checks. A representative payee cannot manage other forms of income or sell stocks, bonds, or real estate. This means that a representative payee is useful only if your monthly needs can be covered by the Social Security or Supplemental Security Income checks. If pension income or holdings in a bank account need to be tapped, a representative payee is not a viable option and a guardian may have to be appointed by a judge to manage your affairs.

CHAPTER

11

Resources

This chapter lists a variety of sources of information and assistance with regard to the rights of the elderly. In many cases, you will be able to make a toll-free call to the agencies and organizations listed. Be sure to keep copies of your correspondence and a record of your calls (when you called, whom you talked to, result).

ATTORNEYS AND GERIATRIC CARE MANAGERS

Two kinds of professionals who may be helpful to readers of this book are elder law attorneys and professional geriatric care managers.

231

Elder law attorneys are lawyers who practice trusts and estates law and who have specialized in laws that pertain to long-term care, Medicare and Medicaid, and guardianship. Most are members of the National Academy of Elder Law Attorneys (NAELA). They have developed standards for the practice of elder law and keep each other informed about important changes in the law.

Professional geriatric care managers are often trained as social workers, nurses, psychologists, or financial planners. They are knowledgeable about local resources, such as home care agencies, nursing homes, doctors who will make house visits, geriatric clinics in hospitals, recreation programs, and other support services that can help to keep an elderly patient safe at home. They often can look after your monthly cash flow, help you apply for public benefits, escort you to the doctor, make appointments for other needed services, and monitor the care that you receive. If your family lives far away, a care manager can be a reliable source of help.

When you choose an attorney or a geriatric care manager, you should make sure that the person you choose is thoroughly familiar with long-term care policies and the Medicaid program in your state. Arrange a preliminary interview before you commit yourself. Don't hesitate to ask in advance about the cost of the services you are interested in. It may be useful to write out a list of the questions you want answered.

Resources

AGENCIES ON AGING

ALABAMA
Commission on Aging
770 Washington Avenue
Suite 470
P.O. Box 301851
Montgomery, AL 36130
1-800-243-5463
(334) 242-5743

ALASKA
Older Alaskans Commission
P.O. Box 110209
Juneau, AK 99811-0209
(907) 465-3250

AMERICAN SAMOA
Territorial Admin. on Aging
Government of American
  Samoa
Pago Pago, AS 96799
(684) 633-1252

ARIZONA
Dept. of Economic Security
Aging & Adult Administration
1789 W. Jefferson Street
Phoenix, AZ 85007
(602) 542-4446

ARKANSAS
Division of Aging and Adult
  Services
1417 Donaghey Plaza South
P.O. Box 1437/Slot 1412
Little Rock, AR 72203-1437
(501) 682-2441

CALIFORNIA
Department of Aging
1600 K Street
Sacramento, CA 95814
(916) 322-3887

COLORADO
Aging and Adult Services
Dept. of Social Services
1517 Sherman St., 4th Fl.
Denver, CO 80203-1714
(303) 866-3851

**COMMONWEALTH OF
THE NORTHERN
MARIANA ISLANDS**
Department of Community
  and Cultural Affairs
  Civic Center
Commonwealth of the
  Northern Mariana Islands
Saipan, CM 96950
(607) 234-6011

CONNECTICUT
Elderly Services Division
175 Main Street
Hartford, CT 06106
1-800-443-9946
(203) 566-7772

DELAWARE
Division of Aging
Dept. of Health & Social
  Services
1901 N. DuPont Highway
2nd Fl. Annex Admin. Bldg.
New Castle, DE 19720
(302) 577-4791

DISTRICT OF
COLUMBIA
Office on Aging
441 4th Street NW
9th Floor
Washington, D.C. 20001
(202) 724-5626
(202) 724-5622

FEDERATED STATES OF
MICRONESIA
State Agency on Aging
Office of Health Services
Ponape, E.C.I. 96941

FLORIDA
Department of Elder Affairs
1317 Winewood Boulevard
Building 1, Room 317
Tallahassee, FL 32399-0700
(904) 922-5297

GEORGIA
Division of Aging Services
Dept. of Human Resources
2 Peachtree St., NW, Rm
  18.403
Atlanta, GA 30303
(404) 657-5258

GUAM
Division of Senior Citizens
Dept. of Public Health and
  Social Services
P.O. Box 2816
Agana, Guam 96910
011 (671) 632-4141

HAWAII
Executive Office on Aging
335 Merchant Street
Room 241
Honolulu, HI 96813
(808) 586-0100

IDAHO
Office on Aging
Statehouse, Room 108
Boise, ID 83720
(208) 334-3833

ILLINOIS
Department on Aging
421 E. Capitol Avenue
Springfield, IL 62701
(217) 785-3356

INDIANA
Div. of Aging & Home
  Services
402 W. Washington Street
P.O. Box 7083
Indianapolis, IN 46207-7083
1-800-545-7763
(317) 232-7020

IOWA
Dept. of Elder Affairs
Jewett Bldg., Suite 236
914 Grand Avenue
Des Moines, IA 50309
(515) 281-5187

KANSAS
Department on Aging
150-S. Docking State Office
  Building
915 S.W. Harrison
Topeka, KS 66612-1500
(913) 296-4986

KENTUCKY
Division of Aging Services
Cabinet for Human
  Resources
275 E. Main St.,
5th Floor, West
Frankfort, KY 40621
(502) 564-6930

LOUISIANA
Governor's Office of Elderly
  Affairs
4550 N. Boulevard
P.O. Box 80374
Baton Rouge, LA 70896-
  0374
(504) 925-1700

MAINE
Bureau of Elder and Adult
  Services
State House, Station 11
Augusta, ME 04333
(207) 624-5335

MARYLAND
Office on Aging
301 W. Preston Street
Room 1004
Baltimore, MD 21201
(410) 225-1102

MASSACHUSETTS
Executive Office of Elder
    Affairs
1 Ashburton Place, 5th Floor
Boston, MA 02108
1-800-882-2003
(617) 727-7750

MICHIGAN
Office of Services to the
    Aging
611 W. Ottawa Street
P.O. Box 30026
Lansing, MI 48909
(517) 373-8230

MINNESOTA
Board of Aging
Human Services Building
4th Floor
444 Lafayette Road
St. Paul, MN 55155-3843
(612) 296-2770

MISSISSIPPI
Div. of Aging & Adult
    Services
750 N. State Street
Jackson, MS 39202
1-800-948-3090
(610) 359-4929

MISSOURI
Division of Aging
Dept. of Social Services
P.O. Box 1337
615 Howerton Court
Jefferson City, MO 65102-
    1337
(314) 751-3082

MONTANA
Office on Aging
48 N. Last Chance Gulch
P.O. Box 8005
Helena, MT 59620
1-800-332-2272
(406) 444-5900

NEBRASKA
Department on Aging
State Office Building
301 Centennial Mall South
Lincoln, NE 68509-5044
(402) 471-2306

NEVADA
Dept. of Human Resources
Division for Aging Services
340 N. 11th St., Suite 114
Las Vegas, NV 89101
(702) 486-3545

NEW HAMPSHIRE
Dept. of Health & Human
  Services
Div. of Elderly & Adult
  Services
State Office Park South
115 Pleasant Street
Annex Building No. 1
Concord, NH 03301
(603) 271-4680

NEW JERSEY
Dept. of Community Affairs
Division on Aging
101 S. Broad Street
CN 807
Trenton, NJ 08625-0807
1-800-792-8820
(609) 984-3951

NEW MEXICO
State Agency on Aging
La Villa Rivera Bldg.
224 E. Palace Ave.
Santa Fe, NM 87501
1-800-432-2080
(505) 827-7640

NEW YORK
State Office for the Aging
2 Empire State Plaza
Albany, NY 12223-0001
1-800-342-9871
(518) 474-5371

NORTH CAROLINA
Division of Aging
693 Palmer Drive
Caller Box 29531
Raleigh, NC 27626-0531
(919) 733-3983

NORTH DAKOTA
Dept. of Human Services
Aging Services Division
P.O. Box 7070
Bismarck, ND 58507-7070
(701) 328-2577
1-800-755-8521

OHIO
Department of Aging
50 W. Broad Street
9th Floor
Columbus, OH 43215-5928
(614) 466-1221
1-800-282-1206

OKLAHOMA
Dept. of Human Services
Aging Services Division
312 NE 28th Street
Oklahoma City, OK 73125
(405) 521-2327

OREGON
Dept. of Human Resources
Senior & Disabled Services
 Div.
500 Summer St., NE, 2nd
 Floor
Salem, OR 97310-1015
1-800-232-3020
(503) 945-5811

PALAU
State Agency on Aging
Dept. of Social Services
Republic of Palau
Koror, Palau 96940

PENNSYLVANIA
Department of Aging
400 Market Street
State Office Building
Harrisburg, PA 17101
(717) 783-1550
1-800-783-7067

PUERTO RICO
Governor's Office of Elderly
 Affairs
Gericulture Commission
Box 11398
Santurce, PR 00910
(809) 722-2429

REPUBLIC OF
MARSHALL ISLANDS
State Agency on Aging
Dept. of Social Services
Republic of Marshall Islands
Marjuro, Marshall Islands
96960

RHODE ISLAND
Dept. of Elderly Affairs
160 Pine Street
Providence, RI 02903
(401) 277-2858
SOUTH CAROLINA
Division on Aging
202 Arbor Lake Drive
Suite 301
Columbia, SC 29223-4554
(803) 737-7500

SOUTH DAKOTA
Office of Adult Services and
 Aging
700 Governors Drive
Pierre, SD 57501-2291
(605) 773-3656

TENNESSEE
Commission on Aging
500 Deaderick Street
9th Floor
Nashville, TN 37243-0860
(615) 741-2056

TEXAS
Department on Aging
P.O. Box 12786 (78711)
1949 IH 35 South
Austin, TX 78741
(512) 444-2727
1-800-252-9240

UTAH
Division of Aging and Adult
 Services
120 North 200 West
P.O. Box 45500
Salt Lake City, UT 84103
(801) 538-3910
1-800-606-0608

VERMONT
Dept. of Aging & Disabilities
Waterbury Complex
103 S. Main Street
Waterbury, VT 05671-2301
(802) 241-2400

VIRGINIA
Dept. for the Aging
700 Centre, 10th Floor
700 E. Franklin Street
Richmond, VA 23219-2327
1-800-552-4464
(804) 225-2271

VIRGIN ISLANDS
Senior Citizen Affairs Div.
Dept. of Human Services
19 Estate Diamond
Fredericksted
St. Croix, VI 00840
(809) 772-0930

WASHINGTON
Aging & Adult Services
 Admin.
Dept. of Social & Health
 Services
P.O. Box 45050
Olympia, WA 98504-5050
(360) 586-3768

WEST VIRGINIA
Commission on Aging
State Capitol Complex
Holly Grove
1900 Kanawha Blvd., East
Charleston, WV 25305-0160
(304) 558-3317

WISCONSIN
Board on Aging and Long-
Term Care
214 N. Hamilton St.
Madison, WI 53703
1-800-242-1060
(608) 266-8944

WYOMING
Division on Aging
Hathaway Building
2300 Capitol Avenue,
Rm. 139
Chyenne, WY 82002
1-800-442-2766
(307) 777-7986

AARP AREA AND STATE OFFICES

For information about AARP membership and national activities and services, write to AARP Headquarters, 601 E Street, NW, Washington, DC 20049, or call (202) 434-AARP. For information about AARP programs, chapters, and other activities in your state or community, contact the Area or state office below that serves your state.

Resources

Area 1 Office
CT,MA,ME,NH,NJ,NY,RI,
VT
116 Huntington Avenue
9th Floor
Boston, MA 02116
(617) 424-0400

New York State Office
919 Third Avenue
9th Floor
New York, NY 10022
(212) 758-1411

Area 3 Office
DC,DE,KY,MD,NC,PA,VA,
WV
1600 Duke Street
2nd Floor
Alexandria, VA 22314
(703) 739-9220

Pennsylvania State Office
225 Market Street
Suite 502
Harrisburg, PA 17101
(717) 238-2277

Area 4 Office
AL,FL,GA,MS,PR,SC,TN,VI
999 Peachtree Street, NE
Suite 1650
Atlanta, GA 30309
(404) 888-0077

Florida State Office
9600 Koger Blvd.
Suite 100
St. Petersburg, FL 33702
(813) 576-1155

Area 5 Office
IL,IN,MI,OH,WI
8750 West Bryn Mawr Avenue
Suite 600
Chicago, IL 60631
(312) 714-9800

Ohio State Office
7 South High Street
Columbus, OH 43215
(614) 224-9800

Area 6 Office
IA,KS,MN,MO,NE
1901 West 47th Place
Suite 104
Westwood, KS 66205
(913) 831-6000

Area 7 Office
AR,LA,NM,OK,TX
8144 Walnut Hill Lane
Suite 700 LB-39
Dallas, TX 75231
(214) 265-4060

Area 8 Office
CO,MT,ND,SD,UT,WY
6975 Union Park Center
Suite 320
Midvale, UT 84047
(801) 561-1037

Colorado State Office
1301 Pennsylvania Street
Suite 200
Denver, CO 80203
(303) 830-2277

Area 9 Office
AZ,CA,HI,NV
4201 Long Beach Blvd.
Suite 422
Long Beach, CA 90807
(310) 427-9611

California State Office
980 - 9th Street
Suite 700
Sacramento, CA 95814
(916) 446-2277

Area 10 Office
AK,ID,OR,WA
9750 Third Avenue, NE
Suite 400
Seattle, WA 98115
(206) 526-7918

INSURANCE DEPARTMENTS

ALABAMA
Insurance Department
Consumer Service Division
135 South Union Street
P.O. Box 303351
Montgomery, AL 36130-3351
(334) 269-3550

ALASKA
Division of Insurance
800 E. Dimond, Suite 560
Anchorage, AK 99515
(907) 349-1230

AMERICAN SAMOA
Insurance Department
Office of the Governor
Pago Pago, AS 96799
011-684/633-4116

ARIZONA
Insurance Department
Consumer Affairs Division
2910 N. 44th St.
Phoenix, AZ 85018
(602) 912-8444

ARKANSAS
Insurance Department
Seniors Insurance Network
1123 S. University Avenue
400 University Tower Bldg.
Little Rock, AR 72204-1699
(501) 686-2940
1-800-852-5494

CALIFORNIA
Insurance Department
Consumer Services Div.
Ronald Reagan Building
300 S. Spring Street
Los Angeles, CA 90013
(213) 897-8921

COLORADO
Insurance Division
1560 Broadway, Suite 850
Denver, CO 80202
(303) 894-7499, ext. 356

CONNECTICUT
Insurance Department
P.O. Box 816
Hartford, CT 06142-0816
(203) 297-3800

DELAWARE
Insurance Department
Rodney Building
841 Silver Lake Blvd.
Dover, DE 19904
(302) 739-4251
1-800-282-8611

**DISTRICT OF COLUM-
   BIA (Wash. DC)**
Insurance Department
441 4th Street, NW
  Suite 850 North
Washington, DC 20001-7200
(202) 727-8000

FLORIDA
Department of Insurance
200 E. Gaines Street
Tallahassee, FL 32399-0300
(904) 922-3100

GEORGIA
Insurance Department
2 Martin L. King, Jr. Drive
716 West Tower
Atlanta, GA 30334
(404) 656-2056

GUAM
Insurance Department
Department of Revenue &
    Taxation
378 Chalan San Antonio
Tamuning, Guam 96911
011 (671) 477-5144

HAWAII
Dept. of Commerce and
    Consumer Affairs
Insurance Division
P.O. Box 3614
Honolulu, HI 96811
(808) 586-2790

IDAHO
Insurance Department
SHIBA Program
700 W. State St., 3rd Fl.
Boise, ID 83720
(208) 334-4350

ILLINOIS
Insurance Department
320 W. Washington Street
4th Floor
Springfield, IL 62767
(217) 782-4515

INDIANA
Insurance Department
311 W. Washington Street
Suite 300
Indianapolis, IN 46204
1-800-622-4461
(317) 232-2395

IOWA
Insurance Division
Lucas State Office Bldg.
E. 12th & Grand Streets
6th Floor
Des Moines, IA 50319
(515) 281-5705

KANSAS
Insurance Department
420 S.W. 9th Street
Topeka, KS 66612
(913) 296-3071
1-800-432-2484

Resources

KENTUCKY
Insurance Department
215 W. Main Street
P.O. Box 517
Frankfort, KY 40602
(502) 564-3630

LOUISIANA
Senior Health Insurance
  Information   Program
(SHIIP)
Insurance Department
P.O. Box 94214
Baton Rouge, LA 70804-
  9214
(504) 342-5301
1-800-259-5301

MAINE
Bureau of Insurance
Consumer Division
State House, Station 34
Augusta, ME 04333
(207) 582-8707

MARYLAND
Insurance Administration
Complaints and Investigation
  Unit - Life & Health
501 St. Paul Place
Baltimore, MD 21202-2272
(410) 333-2793
(410) 333-2770

MASSACHUSETTS
Insurance Division
Consumer Services Section
470 Atlantic Avenue
Boston, MA 02210-2223
(617) 521-7777

MICHIGAN
Insurance Bureau
P.O. Box 30220
Lansing, MI 48909
(517) 373-0240 (Gen.
  Assistance)
(517) 335-1702 (Senior
  Issues)

MINNESOTA
Insurance Department
Department of Commerce
133 E. 7th Street
St. Paul, MN 55101-2362
(612) 296-4026

MISSISSIPPI
Insurance Department
Consumer Assistance Division
P.O. Box 79
Jackson, MS 39205
(601) 359-3569

245

MISSOURI
Department of Insurance
Consumer Services Section
P.O. Box 690
Jefferson City, MO 65102-
  0690
1-800-726-7390
(314) 751-2640

MONTANA
Insurance Department
126 N. Sanders
Mitchell Bldg., Rm. 270
P.O. Box 4009
Helena, MT 59601
(406) 444-2040

NEBRASKA
Insurance Department
Terminal Building
941 "O" St., Suite 400
Lincoln, NE 68508
(402) 471-2201

NEVADA
Department of Business &
  Industry
Division of Insurance
1665 Hot Springs Road,
  Ste. 152
Carson City, NV 89710
(702) 687-4270
1-800-992-0900

NEW HAMPSHIRE
Insurance Department
Life and Health Division
169 Manchester St.
Concord, NH 03301
(603) 271-2261
1-800-852-3416

NEW JERSEY
Insurance Department
20 West State Street
Roebling Building
CN 325
Trenton, NJ 08625
(609) 292-5363

NEW MEXICO
Insurance Department
P.O. Drawer 1269
Santa Fe, NM 87504-1269
(505) 827-4500

NEW YORK
Insurance Department
160 West Broadway
New York, NY 10013
(212) 602-0203
Outside of New York City:
1-800-342-3736

NORTH CAROLINA
Insurance Department
Seniors' Health Insurance
 Information   Program
(SHIIP)
P.O. Box 26387
Raleigh, NC 27611
(919) 733-0111 (SHIIP)
1-800-662-7777 (Consumer
 Services)

NORTH DAKOTA
Insurance Department
Capitol Bldg., 5th Fl.
600 E. Boulevard
Bismarck, ND 58505-0320
1-800-247-0560
(701) 328-2440

OHIO
Insurance Department
Consumer Services Division
2100 Stella Court
Columbus, OH 43215-1067
1-800-686-1526
(614) 644-2673

OKLAHOMA
Insurance Department
P.O. Box 53408
Oklahoma City, OK 73152-
 3408
(405) 521-6628

OREGON
Dept. of Consumer
 & Business Services
Senior Health Insurance
 Benefits Assistance
470 Labor & Industries Bldg.
Salem, OR 97310
(503) 378-4484
1-800-722-4134

PENNSYLVANIA
Insurance Department
Consumer Services Bureau
1321 Strawberry Square
Harrisburg, PA 17120
(717) 787-2317

PUERTO RICO
Office of the Commissioner
 of Insurance
P.O. Box 8330
San Juan, PR 00910-8330
(809) 722-8686

RHODE ISLAND
Insurance Division
233 Richmond St., Suite 233
Providence, RI 02903-4233
(401) 277-2223

SOUTH CAROLINA
Department of Insurance
Consumer Services Section
P.O. Box 100105
Columbia, SC 29202-3105
(803) 737-6180
1-800-768-3467

SOUTH DAKOTA
Insurance Department
500 E. Capitol Avenue
Pierre, SD 57501-5070
(605) 773-3563

TENNESSEE
Dept. of Commerce & Insurance
Insurance Assistance Office
4th Floor
500 James Robertson Pkwy.
Nashville, TN 37243
1-800-525-2816
(615) 741-4955

TEXAS
Department of Insurance
Complaints Resolution, MC
111-1A
333 Guadalupe St., P.O. Box
149091
Austin, TX 78714-9091
(512) 463-6500
1-800-252-3439

UTAH
Insurance Department
Consumer Services
3110 State Office Bldg.
Salt Lake City, UT 84114-
6901
1-800-429-3805
(801) 538-3805

VERMONT
Dept. of Banking & Insurance
Consumer Complaint
Division
89 Main Street, Drawer 20
Montpelier, VT 05620-3101
(802) 828-3302

VIRGINIA
Bureau of Insurance
Consumer Services Division
1300 E. Main Street
P.O. Box 1157
Richmond, VA 23209
(804) 371-9741
1-800-552-7945

VIRGIN ISLANDS
Insurance Department
Kongens Gade No. 18
St. Thomas, VI 00802
(809) 774-2991

WASHINGTON
Insurance Department
4224 6th Ave., SE, Bldg. 4
P.O. Box 40256
Lacey, WA 98504-0256
1-800-562-6900
(206) 753-7300

WEST VIRGINIA
Insurance Department
Consumer Service Division
2019 Washington St., E.
Charleston, WV 25305
(304) 558-3386
1-800-642-9004
1-800-435-7381
(TDD/Hearing Impaired)

WISCONSIN
Insurance Department
Complaints Dept.
P.O. Box 7873
Madison, WI 53707
1-800-236-8517
(608) 266-0103

WYOMING
Insurance Department
Herschler Building
122 W. 25th Street
Cheyenne, WY 82002
1-800-438-5768
(307) 777-7401

INSURANCE COUNSELING

ALABAMA
1-800-243-5463
(307) 777-7401

ALASKA
1-800-478-6065
(907) 562-7249

ARIZONA
1-800-432-4040
(602) 542-6595

ARKANSAS
1-800-852-5494
(501) 686-2940

CALIFORNIA
1-800-927-4357
(916) 323-7315

COLORADO
1-800-544-9181
(303) 894-7499
Ext. 356

CONNECTICUT
1-800-443-9946

DELAWARE
1-800-336-9500

DISTRICT OF
  COLUMBIA
(202) 994-7463

FLORIDA
(904) 922-2073

GEORGIA
1-800-669-8387

HAWAII
(808) 586-0100

IDAHO
S.W.-1-800-247-4422
N.-1-800-488-5725
S.E.-1-800-488-5764
C.-1-800-488-5731

ILLINOIS
1-800-548-9034

INDIANA
1-800-452-4800

IOWA
(515) 281-5705

KANSAS
1-800-432-3535

KENTUCKY
1-800-372-2973

LOUISIANA
1-800-259-5301
(504) 342-5301

MAINE
1-800-750-5353
(207) 624-5335

MARYLAND
1-800-243-3425

MASSACHUSETTS
1-800-882-2003
(617) 727-7750

MICHIGAN
(517) 373-8230

MINNESOTA
1-800-882-6262

MISSISSIPPI
1-800-948-3090

MISSOURI
1-800-390-3330

MONTANA
1-800-332-2272

NEBRASKA
(402) 471-4506

NEVADA
1-800-307-4444
(702) 367-1218

NEW HAMPSHIRE
1-800-852-3388
(603) 271-4642

NEW JERSEY
1-800-792-8820

NEW MEXICO
1-800-432-2080

NEW YORK
1-800-333-4114
NY City- 212-869-3850

NORTH CAROLINA
1-800-443-9354

NORTH DAKOTA
1-800-247-0560

OHIO
1-800-686-1578

OKLAHOMA
(405) 521-6628

OREGON
1-800-772-4134

PENNSYLVANIA
1-800-783-7067
(717) 783-8975

PUERTO RICO
(809) 721-5710

RHODE ISLAND
1-800-322-2880

SOUTH CAROLINA
1-800-868-9095

SOUTH DAKOTA
(605) 773-3656

TENNESSEE
1-800-525-2816

TEXAS
1-800-252-3439

UTAH
1-800-606-0608
(801) 538-3910

VERMONT
1-800-828-3302

VIRGINIA
1-800-552-4464

VIRGIN ISLANDS
(809) 774-2991

WASHINGTON
1-800-397-4422

WEST VIRGINIA
(304) 558-3317
WISCONSIN
1-800-242-1060

WYOMING
1-800-438-5768

NATIONAL CITIZENS
  COALITION FOR
  NURSING HOME RE-
  FORM
(202) 393-2018

Resources

LONG-TERM CARE OMBUDSMAN PROGRAMS

ALABAMA
State LTC Ombudsman
Tel: (205) 242-5743
Fax: (205) 242-5594

ALASKA
State LTC Ombudsman
Tel: (907) 279-2232
Fax: (907) 562-3040

ARIZONA
State LTC Ombudsman
Tel: (602) 542-4446
Fax: (602) 542-6575

ARKANSAS
State LTC Ombudsman
Tel: (501) 682-2441
Fax: (501) 682-5155

CALIFORNIA
State LTC Ombudsman
Tel: (916) 323-6681
FAX: (916) 323-7299
COLORADO
State LTC Ombudsman
Tel: (303) 722-0300
Fax: (303) 722-0720

CONNECTICUT
State LTC Ombudsman
Tel: (203) 424-5242
Fax: (203) 424-4966

DELAWARE
State LTC Ombudsman
Tel: (302) 422-1386
Fax: (302) 422-1519

DISTRICT OF COLUMBIA
State LTC Ombudsman
Office
Tel: (202) 662-4933
Fax: (202) 434-6464

FLORIDA
State LTC Ombudsman
Tel: (904) 488-6190
Fax: (904) 488-5657

GEORGIA
LTC State Ombudsman
Tel: (404) 657-5319
Fax: (404) 657-5285

HAWAII
State LTC Ombudsman
Tel: (808) 586-0100
Fax: (808) 586-0185

IOWA
State LTC Ombudsman
Tel: (515) 281-5187
Fax: (515) 281-4036

IDAHO
State Ombudsman for
the Elderly
Tel: (208) 334-2220
Fax: (208) 334-3033

ILLINOIS
State LTC Ombudsmen
Tel: (217) 785-3140
INDIANA
State LTC Ombudsman
Tel: (317) 232-7134
Fax: (317) 232-1240

KANSAS
State LTC Ombudsman
Tel: (913) 296-4986
Fax: (913) 296-0256

KENTUCKY
State LTC Ombudsman
Office
Tel: (502) 564-6930
Fax: (502) 564-4595

LOUISIANA
State LTC Ombudsman
Tel: (504) 925-1700
Fax: (504) 925-1749

MAINE
State LTC Ombudsman
Tel: (207) 287-4056
Fax: (207) 287-1178

MARYLAND
State LTC Ombudsman
Tel: (410) 225-1100
Fax: (410) 333-7943

MASSACHUSETTS
State LTC Ombudsman
Tel: (617) 727-7750
Fax: (617) 727-9368

MICHIGAN
State LTC Ombudsman
Tel: (517) 336-6753
Fax: (517) 336-7718

MINNESOTA
State LTC Ombudsman
Tel: (612) 296-0382
Fax: (612) 297-7855

MISSISSIPPI
State LTC Ombudsman
Tel: (601) 359-4929
Fax: (601) 359-4970

MISSOURI
State LTC Ombudsman
Tel: (314) 751-3082
Fax: (314) 751-8687

MONTANA
State LTC Ombudsman
Tel: (406) 444-5900
Fax: (406) 444-5956

NEBRASKA
State LTC Ombudsman
Tel: (402) 471-2306
Fax: (402) 471-4619

NORTH CAROLINA
State LTC Ombudsman
Tel: (919) 733-3983
Fax: (919) 733-0443

NORTH DAKOTA
State LTC Ombudsman
Tel: (701) 224-2577
Fax: (701) 221-5466

NEVADA
State LTC Ombudsman
Tel: (702) 486-3545

NEW HAMPSHIRE
State LTC Ombudsman
Tel: (603) 271-4375
Fax: (603) 271-4643

NEW JERSEY
Ombudsman Office for Inst.
 Elderly
Tel: (609) 292-8016
Fax: (609) 984-1810

NEW MEXICO
State LTC Ombudsman
Tel: (505) 827-7640
Fax: (505) 827-7649

NEW YORK
State LTC Ombudsman
Tel: (518) 474-7329
Fax: (518) 474-0608

OHIO
State LTC Ombudsman
Tel: (614) 466-1221
Fax: (614) 466-5741

OKLAHOMA
State LTC Ombudsman
Tel: (405) 521-6734
Fax: (405) 521-2086

OREGON
State LTC Ombudsman
Tel: (503) 378-6533
Fax: (503) 373-0852

PENNSYLVANIA
State LTC Ombudsman
Tel: (717) 783-7247
Fax: (717) 783-6842

PUERTO RICO
State LTC Ombudsman
Tel: (809) 721-8225
Fax: (809) 721-3510

RHODE ISLAND
State LTC Ombudsman
Tel: (401) 277-2858
Fax: (401) 277-2130

SOUTH CAROLINA
State LTC Ombudsman
Tel: (803) 737-7500
Fax: (803) 737-7501

SOUTH DAKOTA
State LTC Ombudsman
Tel: (605) 773-3656
Fax: (605) 773-4855

TENNESSEE
State LTC Ombudsman
Tel: (615) 741-2056
Fax: (615) 741-3309

TEXAS
State LTC Ombudsman
Tel: (512) 444-2727
Fax: (512) 440-5290

UTAH
State LTC Ombudsman
Tel: (801) 538-3924
Fax: (801) 538-4016

VERMONT
State LTC Ombudsman
Tel: (802) 748-8721
Fax: (802) 748-4612

VIRGINIA
State LTC Ombudsman
  Program
Tel: (804) 225-2271
Fax: (804) 371-8381

Resources

WASHINGTON
State LTC Ombudsman
Tel: (206) 838-6810
Fax: (206) 874-7831

WEST VIRGINIA
State LTC Ombudsman
Office
Tel: (304) 558-3371
Fax: (304) 558-0004

WISCONSIN
State LTC Ombudsman
Tel: (608) 266-8944
Fax: (608) 261-6570

WYOMING
State LTC Ombudsman
Tel: (307) 322-5553

MEDICAID OFFICES

ALABAMA
Alabama Medicaid Agency
Medicaid Eligibility Division
2388 Fairlane Drive
Montgomery, AL 36130
Phone: (205) 242-1708

ALASKA
Alaska Medical Assistance
  Division
Medical Services Division
Health and Human Services
  Dept.
Alaska Office Bldg.
P.O. Box 110660
Juneau, AK 99811-0660
Phone: (907) 465-3355
Fax: (907) 465-2204

AMERICAN SAMOA
American Samoa Medical
  Services
LBJ Tropical Medical Center
Fagaalu, AS 96799
Phone: (684) 633-5743
Fax: (684) 633-1869

ARIZONA
Arizona Health Care Cost
  Containment Systems
801 East Jefferson St.
Phoenix, AZ 85034
Phone: (602) 234-5522

ARKANSAS
Arkansas Economic and Medical Services Division
Human Services Department
Donaghey Bldg., Suite 329
P.O. Box 1437
Little Rock, AR 72203-1437
Phone: (501) 682-8375
Fax: (501) 682-6571

CALIFORNIA
California Health Services Dept.
714/744 P. Street
P.O. Box 942732
Sacramento, CA 94234-7320
Phone: (916) 322-0391
Fax: (916) 657-1156

COLORADO
Colorado Health and Medical Services
Social Services Department
1575 Sherman Street
Denver, CO 80203-1714
Phone: (303) 866-6092
Fax: (303) 866-4214

CONNECTICUT
Connecticut Health Care Financing Department
Social Services Department
110 Bartholomew Avenue
Hartford, CT 06106
Phone: (203) 566-2759
Fax: (203) 566-6478

DELAWARE
Delaware Health and Social Services Department
1901 North DuPont Hwy.
New Castle, DE 19720
Phone: (302) 577-4400
Fax: (302) 577-4510

DISTRICT OF COLUMBIA
District of Columbia Health Care Financing Office
Human Services Department
801 North Capital St., N.E.
Washington, DC 20002
Phone: (202) 727-0735
Fax: (202) 724-4346

FLORIDA
Florida Health and Rehabilitative Services Department
1317 Winewood Blvd.
Tallahassee, FL 32399-0700
Phone: (904) 487-1111
Fax: (904) 487-4682

GEORGIA
Georgia Medical Assistance
  Department
2 Martin Luther King, Jr.
  Dr., S.E.
West Tower
Atlanta, GA 30334
Phone: (404) 656-2515
Fax: (404) 651-6880

GUAM
Guam Public Health and So-
  cial Services Department
P.O. Box 2816
Agana, GU 96910
Phone: (671) 734-7399
Fax: (671) 734-5910

HAWAII
Hawaii Health Care
  Administration
Human Services Department
P.O. Box 339
Honolulu, HI 96809-0339
Phone: (808) 586-5391
Fax: (808) 586-4890

IDAHO
Idaho Health Division
Health and Welfare Depart-
  ment
Towers Bldg.
450 West State Street
Boise, ID 83720-5450
Phone: (208) 334-5945
Fax: (208) 334-6581

ILLINOIS
Illinois Public Aid
  Department
100 South Grand Ave.,
3rd Fl. East
Springfield, IL 62762
Phone: (217) 782-2570
Fax: (217) 782-1199

INDIANA
Indiana Medicaid Policy and
  Planning Office
Family and Social Services
  Administration
402 West Washington St., Rm.
  W341
Indianapolis, IN 46204-7083
Phone: (317) 233-4448
Fax: (317) 233-4693

IOWA
Iowa Medical Services
  Division
Human Services Department
Hoover Bldg.
Des Moines, IA 50319-0114
Phone: (515) 281-8794
Fax: (515) 281-4597

KANSAS
Kansas Income Support and
  Medical Services Office
Social and Rehab.
  Services Dept.
Docking State Office Bldg.
915 S.W. Harrision St.,
6th Fl.
Topeka, KS 66612
Phone: (913) 296-3981
Fax: (913) 296-1158

KENTUCKY
Medicaid Services Dept.
Human Resources Cabinet
275 East Main Street
Frankfort, KY 40621-0001
Phone: (502) 564-4321

LOUISIANA
Louisiana Health Services
  Financing Bureau
Health and Hospitals
  Department
P.O. Box 629
Baton Rouge, LA 70821-
  0629
Phone: (504) 342-3891
Fax: (504) 342-9508

MAINE
Maine Medical Program/Eli-
  gibility and Supplemental
  Security Income Division
Income Maintenance Bureau
State House Station #11
Augusta, ME 04333
Phone: (207) 287-5098
Fax: (207) 626-5555

MARYLAND
Maryland Health Care Access
  and Cost Commission
4201 Patterson Ave., 5th Fl.
Baltimore, MD 21215
Phone: (410) 764-3460
Fax: (410) 764-5987

MASSACHUSETTS
Massachusetts Public Welfare
  Dept./Consumer Affairs
  and Business
Regulation Executive Office
600 Washington St.
Boston, MA 02111
Phone: (617) 348-8400
Fax: (617) 727-0166

MICHIGAN
Michigan Medical Services
  Administration
Social Services Department
235 South Grand
P.O. Box 30037
Lansing, MI 48909
Phone: (517) 335-5453
Fax: (517) 335-8471

MINNESOTA
Minnesota Health Care Ad-
  ministration
Human Services Department
Human Services Bldg.
444 Lafayette Road
St. Paul, MN 55155
Phone: (612) 297-3374
Fax: (612) 296-6244

MISSISSIPPI
Mississippi Health
  Department
P.O. Box 1700
Jackson, MS 39215-1700
Phone: (601) 960-7400
Fax: (601) 960-7948

MISSOURI
Missouri Medical Services
  Division
Social Services Department
221 West High Street
P.O. Box 1527
Jefferson City, MO 65102
Phone: (314) 751-3425
Fax: (314) 751-3203

MONTANA
Montana Medicaid Services
  Division
Social and Rehab. Services
  Dept.
P.O. Box 4210
Helena, MT 59604
Phone: (406) 444-4540
Fax: (406) 444-1970

NEBRASKA
Nebraska Medical Services
  Division
Social Services Department
301 Centennial Mall South
P.O. Box 95026
Lincoln, NE 68509-5026
Phone: (402) 471-9147
Fax: (402) 471-9455

NEVADA
Nevada Health Office
Human Resources
  Department
505 East King St., Rm. 600
Carson City, NV 89710
Phone: (702) 687-4740
Fax: (702) 687-4733
Contact: Yvonne Sylva,
  Administrator

NEW HAMPSHIRE
New Hampshire Medical Ser-
  vices Office
Human Services Division
Health and Human Services
  Dept.
6 Hazen Drive
Concord, NH 03301
Phone: (603) 271-4353
Fax: (603) 271-4727

NEW JERSEY
New Jersey Medical
  Assistance and Health Ser-
  vices Division
Human Services Department
7 Quakerbridge Plaza
CN 712
Trenton, NJ 08625
Phone: (609) 588-2600
Fax: (609) 588-3583

NEW MEXICO
New Mexico Medical Assis-
  tance Division
Human Services Dept.
P.O. Box 2348
Santa Fe, NM 87504-2348
Phone: (505) 827-4323
Fax: (505) 827-7729

NEW YORK
New York Medicaid
  Management Information
  Systems Bureau
Medical Assistance Division
Social Services Department
40 North Pearl St.
Albany, NY 12243
Phone: (518) 474-9069
Fax: (518) 474-7870

NORTH CAROLINA
North Carolina Medical
  Assistance Division
Human Resources
  Department
1985 Umstead Dr.
Raleigh, NC 27603
Phone: (919) 733-2060

NORTH DAKOTA
North Dakota Medical
  Services Office
Human Services Department
State Capitol, Judicial Wing
600 East Boulevard Avenue
Bismarck, ND 58505
Phone: (701) 224-2321
Fax: (701) 224-2359

OHIO
Ohio Medicaid Administra-
  tion Office
Human Services Department
30 East Broad Street
Columbus, OH 43266-0423
Phone: (614) 644-0410
Fax: (614) 752-3986

OKLAHOMA
Oklahoma Medical Services
  Division
Human Services Department
P.O. Box 25352
Oklahoma City, OK 73125
Phone: (405) 557-2539
Fax: (405) 521-6715

OREGON
Oregon Medical Assistance
  Programs Office
Human Resources
  Department
Human Resources Bldg.
500 Summer St., N.E.
Salem, OR 97310
Phone: (503) 945-5772
Fax: (503) 378-2897

PENNSYLVANIA
Pennsylvania Public Welfare
  Department
P.O. Box 2675
Harrisburg, PA 17105
Phone: (717) 787-1870
Fax: (717) 772-2490

RHODE ISLAND
Rhode Island Medical Services Division
Human Services Department
600 New London Avenue
Cranston, RI 02920
Phone: (401) 464-3575
Fax: (401) 464-1876

SOUTH CAROLINA
South Carolina State Health and Human Services Finance Commission
P.O. Box 8206
Columbia, SC 29202-8206
Phone: (803) 253-6100
Fax: (803) 253-4137

SOUTH DAKOTA
South Dakota Medical Services Office
Program Management Division
Social Services Department
700 Governors Dr.
Pierre, SD 57501-2291
Phone: (605) 773-3495
Fax: (605) 773-4855

TENNESSEE
Tennessee Medicaid Bureau/ Health Department
729 Church Street
Nashville, TN 37247-6501
Phone: (615) 741-0213
Fax: (615) 741-0882

TEXAS
Texas Medicaid Office/ Health and Human Services Commission
P.O. Box 13249
Austin, TX 78711
Phone: (512) 502-3200
Fax: (512) 502-3294

UTAH
Utah Medicaid Claims Processing Division
Health Care Financing Division
Health Department
288 North 1460 West
Salt Lake City, UT 84116-0700
Phone: (801) 538-6451
Fax: (801) 538-6694

VERMONT
Vermont Medicaid Division
Social Welfare Department
Human Services Agency
State Complex
103 South Main Street
Waterbury, VT 05676
Phone: (802) 241-2880
Fax: (802) 241-2830

VIRGIN ISLANDS
Virgin Islands Health Dept.
21-22 Kongens Gade
St. Thomas, VI 00802
Phone: (809) 776-8311
Fax: (809) 776-0610
Contact: Alfred Heath,
Commissioner

VIRGINIA
Virginia Medical Assistance
  Services Department
600 East Broad St., Suite 1300
Richmond, VA 23219
Phone: (804) 786-7933
Fax: (804) 225-4512

WASHINGTON
Washington Medical Assis-
  tance Administration
Social and Health Services
  Department
P.O. Box 45010
Olympia, WA 98504-5010
Phone: (206) 752-1777
Fax: (206) 586-5874

WEST VIRGINIA
West Virginia Medicaid Unit
Behavioral Health Services
  Office
Human Resources Bureau
Health and Human Resources
  Dept.
State Capitol Complex
Bldg. 6, Room 617
Charleston, WV 25305
Phone: (304) 558-7867
West Virginia Medical
  Services Office
Administration and Finance
  Bureau
Health and Human Resources
  Dept.
7012 MacCorkle Ave., S.E.
Charleston, WV 25304
Phone: (304) 926-1700

WISCONSIN
Wisconsin Health Care
Financing Bureau
Health Division
Health and Social Services
  Dept.
P.O. Box 7850
Madison, WI 53707
Phone: (608) 266-2522
Fax: (608) 267-2832

WYOMING
Wyoming Health Care Fi-
  nancing Division
Health Department
117 Hathaway Bldg.
Cheyenne, WY 82002
Phone: (307) 777-7531
Fax: (307) 777-7439

MEDICARE CARRIERS

ALABAMA
Medicare/Blue Cross-Blue
  Shield of Alabama
P.O. Box 830140
Birmingham, AL 35283-0140
1-800-292-8855
(205) 988-2244

ALASKA
Medicare/Aetna Life
  Insurance Company
200 S.W. Market Street
P.O. Box 1998
Portland, OR 97207-1988
1-800-452-0125
(503) 222-6831

ARIZONA
Medicare/Aetna Life
  Insurance Company
P.O. Box 37200
Phoenix, AZ 85069
1-800-352-0411
(602) 861-1968

ARKANSAS
Medicare/Arkansas Blue
  Cross & Blue Shield
P.O. Box 1418
Little Rock, AR 72203-1418
1-800-482-5525
(501) 378-2320

CALIFORNIA
Counties of Los Angeles, Or-
ange, San Diego, Ventura,
Imperial, San Luis Obispo,
Santa Barbara:
Medicare/Transamerica Occi-
dental Life Insurance Com-
pany
Box 30540
Los Angeles, CA 90030-0540
1-800-675-2266 or
(213) 748-2311
Rest of State:
Medicare Claims Dept.
Blue Shield of California
Chico, CA 95976
(For area codes 209, 408, 415,
510, 707, 916) call: 1-800-
952-8627 or (916)743-1583
For area codes 213, 310, 619,
714, 805, 818, 909) call: 1-
800-848-7713 or (714) 796-
9393

COLORADO
Medicare/Blue Shield of
North Dakota
Govenor's Center II
600 Grant St., Suite 600
Denver, CO 80203
1-800-247-2267
(701) 282-0691

CONNECTICUT
Medicare/The Travelers
Companies
538 Preston Avenue
P.O. Box 9000
Meriden, CT 06454-9000
1-800-982-6819
Meriden: (203) 237-8592
Hartford: (203) 728-6783

DELAWARE
Xact Medicare Services
P.O. Box 890065
Camp Hill, PA 17089-0065
1-800-851-3535

DISTRICT OF COLUMBIA
Xact Medicare Services
P.O. Box 890065
Camp Hill, PA 17089-0065
1-800-233-1124
FLORIDA
Medicare/Blue Cross & Blue
  Shield of Florida, Inc.
P.O. Box 2360
Jacksonville, FL 32231
For Copies of EXPLANA-
TION OF YOUR MEDI-
CARE PART B notices, re-
quests for MEDPAR directo-
ries, brief claims inquiries
(status or verification of re-
ceipt), and address changes:
1-800-666-7586
(904) 355-8899
For all other Medicare needs:
1-800-333-7586
(904) 355-3680

GEORGIA
Medicare/Aetna Life Insurance Company
P.O. Box 3018
Savannah, GA 31402-3018
1-800-727-0827
(912) 920-2412

HAWAII
Medicare/Aetna Life Insurance Company
P.O. Box 3947
Honolulu, HI 96812
1-800-272-5242
(808) 524-1240

IDAHO
Connecticut General Life Insurance Co.
3150 N. Lakeharbor Lane,
Suite 254
P.O. Box 8048
Boise, ID 83707-6219
1-800-627-2782
(208) 342-7763

ILLINOIS
Medicare Claims/Health Care
  Service Corp.
P.O. Box 4422
Marion, IL 62959
1-800-642-6930
(312) 938-8000

INDIANA
Medicare Part B/AdminaStar
  Federal
P.O. Box 7073
Indianapolis, IN 46207
1-800-622-4792
(317) 842-4151

IOWA
Medicare/IASD Health Services Corp.
(d/b/a Blue Cross & Blue Shield of Iowa)
P.O. Box 9269
Des Moines, IA 50306
1-800-532-1285
(515) 245-4785

KANSAS
Counties of Johnson and Wyandotte:
Medicare/Blue Cross and Blue Shield of Kansas, Inc.
P.O. Box 419840
Kansas City, MO 64141-6840
1-800-892-5900
(816) 561-0900
Rest of state:
Medicare/Blue Cross & Blue Shield of Kansas, Inc.
1133 S.W. Topeka Boulevard
P.O. Box 239
Topeka, KS 66629-0001
1-800-432-3531
(913) 232-3773

KENTUCKY
Administar
P.O. Box 37630
Louisville, KY 40233-7630
1-800-999-7608
(502) 425-6759

LOUISIANA
Arkansas Blue Cross & Blue Shield, Inc.
Medicare Administration
P.O. Box 83830
Baton Rouge, LA 70884-3830
1-800-462-9666
In New Orleans: (504) 529-1494
In Baton Rouge: (504) 927-3490

MAINE
Medicare/C and S Administrative Services
P.O. Box 1000
Hingham, MA 02044-9191
For Nonassigned Claims:
P.O. Box 2222
Hingham, MA 02044-9193
1-800-492-0919
(207) 828-4300

MARYLAND
Counties of Montgomery,
  Prince Georges:
Medicare/Xact Medicare Ser-
  vices
P.O. Box 890065
Camp Hill, PA 17089-0065
1-800-233-1124
Rest of state:
Trail Blazer Enterprises
P.O. Box 5678
Timonium, MD 21094-5678
1-800-492-4795

MASSACHUSETTS
Medicare/C and S Adminis-
  trative Services
P.O. Box 1000
Hingham, MA 02044-9191
For Nonassigned Claims:
P.O. Box 2222
Hingham, MA 02044-9193
1-800-882-1228
(617) 741-3300

MICHIGAN
HCSC
Michigan Medicare Claims
P.O. Box 5544
Marion, Illinois 62959
(313) 225-8200
1-800-482-4045

MINNESOTA
Counties of Anoka, Dakota,
Fillmore, Goodhue, Henne-
pin, Houston, Olmstead,
Ramsey, Wabasha, Washing-
ton, Winona:
Medicare/The Travelers In-
  surance Co.
8120 Penn Avenue South
Bloomington, MN 55431
1-800-352-2762
(612) 884-7171
Rest of state:
Medicare/Blue Cross and
  Blue Shield of Minnesota
P.O. Box 64357
St. Paul, MN 55164
1-800-392-0343
(612) 456-5070

MISSISSIPPI
Medicare/The Travelers Insurance Co.
P.O. Box 22545
Jackson, MS 39225-2545
1-800-682-5417
(601) 956-0372

MISSOURI

Counties of Andrew, Atchison, Bates, Benton, Buchanan, Caldwell, Caroll, Cass, Clay, Clinton, Daviess, De-Kalb, Gentry, Grundy, Harrison, Henry, Holt, Jackson, Johnson, Lafayette, Livingston, Mercer, Nodaway, Pettis, Platte, Ray, St. Clair, Saline, Vernon, Worth:

Medicare/Blue Cross & Blue
  Shield of Kansas, Inc.
P.O. Box 419840
Kansas City, MO 64141-6840
1-800-892-5900
(816) 561-0900

Rest of state:
Medicare/General American
  Life Insurance Co.
P.O. Box 505
St. Louis, MO 63166
1-800-392-3070
(314) 843-8880

MONTANA

Medicare/Blue Cross & Blue
  Shield of Montana, Inc.
2501 Beltview
P.O. Box 4310
Helena, MT 59604
1-800-332-6146
(406) 444-8350

NEBRASKA

The carrier for Nebraska is Blue Cross and Blue Shield of Kansas, Inc.
Claims, should be sent to:
Medicare Part B/Blue Cross/
  Blue Shield of Nebraska
P.O. Box 3106
Omaha, NE 68103-0106
1-800-633-1113

NEVADA

Medicare/Aetna Life Insurance Company
P.O. Box 37230
Phoenix, AZ 85069
1-800-528-0311
(602) 861-1968

NEW HAMPSHIRE

Medicare/C & S Administra-
  tive Services
P.O. Box 1000
Hingham, MA 02044-9191
For Nonassigned Claims:
P.O. Box 2222
Hingham, MA 02044-9193
1-800-447-1142
(207) 828-4300

NEW JERSEY
Xact Medicare Services
P.O. Box 890065
Camp Hill, PA 17089-0065
1-800-462-9306

NEW MEXICO
Medicare/Aetna Life Insurance Company
P.O. Box 25500
Oklahoma City, OK 73125-0500
1-800-423-2925
In Albuquerque:
(505) 821-3350

NEW YORK
Counties of Bronx, Columbia, Delaware, Dutchess, Greene, Kings, Nassau, New York, Orange, Putnam, Richmond, Rockland, Suffolk, Sullivan, Ulster, Westchester:
Medicare B/Empire Blue Cross & Blue Shield
P.O. Box 2280
Peekskill, NY 10566
1-800-442-8430
(516) 244-5100
County of Queens:
Medicare/Group Health, Inc.
P.O. Box 1608
Ansonia Station
New York, NY 10023
(212) 721-1770
Rest of state:
Blue Cross & Blue Shield of Western New York
Upstate Medicare Division-Part B
33 Lewis Rd.
Binghamton, NY 13905-5200
1-800-252-6550

NORTH CAROLINA
Connecticut General Life Insurance Co.
P.O. Box 671
Nashville, TN 37202
1-800-672-3071
(919) 665-0348

NORTH DAKOTA
Medicare/Blue Shield of
  North Dakota
711 2nd Ave., N.
Fargo, ND 58102
1-800-247-2267
(701) 277-2363

OHIO
Medicare/Nationwide Mu-
  tual Insurance Co.
P.O. Box 57
Columbus, OH 43216
1-800-282-0530
(614) 249-7157

OKLAHOMA
Medicare/Aetna Life Insurance Company
701 N.W. 63rd Street
Oklahoma City, OK 73116-
7693
1-800-522-9079
(405) 848-7711

OREGON
Medicare/Aetna Life Insurance Company
200 S.W. Market Street
P.O. Box 1997
Portland, OR 97207-1997
1-800-452-0125
(503) 222-6831

PENNSYLVANIA
Xact Medicare Services
P.O. Box 890065
Camp Hill, PA 17089-0065
1-800-382-1274

RHODE ISLAND
Medicare/Blue Cross & Blue
  Shield of Rhode Island
Inquiry Department
444 Westminster Street
Providence, RI 02903-3279
1-800-662-5170
(401) 861-2273

SOUTH CAROLINA
Palmetto Government Bene-
  fits Administrators
Medicare Part B Operations
P.O. Box 100190
Columbia, SC 29202
1-800-868-2522
(803) 788-3882

273

SOUTH DAKOTA
Medicare Part B/Blue Shield
  of North Dakota
711 2nd Ave., N.
Fargo, ND 58102
1-800-437-4762

TENNESSEE
CIGNA Medicare
P.O. Box 1465
Nashville, TN 37202
1-800-342-8900
(615) 244-5650

TEXAS
Medicare/Blue Cross & Blue
  Shield of Texas, Inc.
P.O. Box 660031
Dallas, TX 75266-0031
1-800-442-2620
(214) 235-3433

UTAH
Medicare/Blue Shield of Utah
P.O. Box 30269
Salt Lake City, UT 84130-
0269
1-800-426-3477
(801) 481-6196

VERMONT
Medicare/C and S Adminis-
  trative Services
P.O. Box 1000
Hingham, MA 02044-9191
For Nonassigned Claims:
P.O. Box 2222
Hingham, MA 02044-9193
1-800-447-1142
(207) 828-4300

VIRGINIA
Counties of Arlington, Fair-
fax; Cities of: Alexandria,
Falls Church, Fairfax:
Xact Medicare Services
P.O. Box 890065
Camp Hill, PA 17089-0065
1-800-233-1124
(717) 763-3601
Rest of state:
Medicare/The Travelers Ins.
  Co.
P.O. Box 26463
Richmond, VA 23261-6463
1-800-552-3423
(804) 330-4786

Resources

WASHINGTON
Aetna Life Insurance Company
Medicare Part B
P.O. Box 91099
Seattle, WA 98111-9199
1-800-372-6604
In Seattle: (206) 621-0359

WEST VIRGINIA
Medicare/Nationwide Mutual Insurance Co.
P.O. Box 57
Columbus, OH 43216
1-800-848-0106
(614) 249-7157

WISCONSIN
Medicare/WPS
Box 1787
Madison, WI 53701
1-800-944-0051
In Madison: (608) 221-3330
TDD 1-800-828-2837

WYOMING
Blue Cross & Blue Shield of North Dakota
P.O. Box 628
Cheyenne, WY 82003
1-800-442-2371
(307) 632-9381

AMERICAN SAMOA
Medicare/Hawaii Medical Service Association
P.O. Box 860
Honolulu, HI 96808
(808) 944-2247

GUAM
Medicare/Aetna Life Insurance Company
P.O. Box 3947
Honolulu, HI 96812
(808) 524-1240

NORTHERN MARIANA ISLANDS
Medicare/Aetna Life Insurance Company
P.O. Box 3947
Honolulu, HI 96812
(808) 524-1240

PUERTO RICO
Medicare/ Triple-S, Inc.
P.O. Box 71391
San Juan, PR 00936-1391
(In St. Thomas) (809) 774-7915
(In St. Croix) (809) 773-9548
1-800-981-7015

VIRGIN ISLANDS
Medicare/Triple-S, Inc
P.O. Box 71391
San Juan, PR 00936-1391
  1-800-474-7448
(In St. Thomas) (809) 774-
  7915
(In St. Croix) (809) 773-9548

MEDICARE PEER REVIEW ORGANIZATIONS (PROs)

PROs can answer questions about the quality of care and access to care in a Medicare-certified facility. PROs cannot answer questions about your bill or about what Medicare covers. For Part A or Part B billing coverage questions, call your Part B carrier or your Part A intermediary.

ALABAMA
Alabama Quality Assurance
  Foundation, Inc.
Suite 200 North
One Perimeter Park South
Birmingham, AL 35243-2327
1-800-760-3540

ALASKA
PRO-WEST
(PRO for Alaska)
Suite 100
10700 Meridan Avenue,
  North
Seattle, WA 98133-9075
1-800-445-6941
In Anchorage dial: 562-2252

* PRO will accept collect calls from out of state on this number.

AMERICAN SAMOA and
GUAM
(see Hawaii)

ARIZONA
Health Services Advisory
  Group, Inc.
301 East Bethany Home
Road, B-157
Phoenix, AZ 85012
1-800-626-1577
In Arizona dial:
1-800-359-9909, or
1-800-223-6693

ARKANSAS
Arkansas Foundation for
  Medical Care, Inc.
P.O. Box 2424
809 Garison Avenue
Fort Smith, AR 72902
1-800-824-7586
In Arkansas: 1-800-272-5528

CALIFORNIA
California Medical Review,
  Inc.
Suite 500
60 Spear Street
San Francisco, CA 94105
1-800-841-1602 (in-state
  only)
(415) 882-5800*

COLORADO
Colorado Foundation for
  Medical Care
2821 South Parker Road
Aurora, CO 88014
1-800-727-7086 (in-state
  only)
(303) 695-3333*

CONNECTICUT
Connecticut Peer Review
  Organization, Inc.
100 Roscommon Drive, Suite
  200
Middletown, CT 06457
1-800-553-7590 (in-state
  only)
(203) 632-2008*

* PRO will accept collect calls from out of state on this number.

DELAWARE
West Virginia Medical
 Institute, Inc.
(PRO for Delaware)
3001 Chesterfield Place
Charleston, WV 25304
1-800-642-8686 ext. 266
In Wilmington: 655-3077

DISTRICT OF COLUM-
BIA
Delmarva Foundation for
 Medical Care, Inc.
(PRO for D.C.)
9240 Centreville Road
Easton, MD 21601
1-800-645-0011
In Maryland: 1-800-492-
 5811

FLORIDA
Florida Medical Quality Insurance, Inc.
1211 N. Westshore Boulevard
Suite 700
Tampa, FL 33607
1-800-844-0795
(813) 281-9024

GEORGIA
Georgia Medical Care
 Foundation
Suite 200
57 Executive Park South
Atlanta, GA 30329
1-800-282-2614 (in-state
 only)
(404) 982-0411

HAWAII
Hawaii Medical Service
 Association
(PRO for American Samoa/
 Guam & Hawaii)
818 Keeaumoku Street
P.O. Box 860
Honolulu, HI 96808-0860
(808) 944-3581*

IDAHO
PRO-WEST
(PRO for Idaho)
Suite 100
10700 Meridan Avenue,
 North
Seattle, WA 98133-9075
1-800-445-6941
(208) 343-4617* (local Boise and
 collect)

* PRO will accept collect calls from out of state on this number.

ILLINOIS
Crescent Counties Foundation for Medical Care
1001 Warrenville Road
Lisle, IL 60532
1-800-647-8089
(708) 769-9600

INDIANA
Indiana Medical Review Organization
2901 Ohio Boulevard
P.O. Box 3713
Terre Haute, IN 47803
1-800-288-1499

IOWA
Iowa Foundation for Medical Care
Suite 350E
6000 Westown Parkway
West Des Moines, IA 50266-7771
1-800-752-7014
(515) 223-2900

KANSAS
The Kansas Foundation for Medical Care, Inc.
2947 S.W. Wanakaker Drive
Topeka, KS 66614
1-800-432-0407 (in-state only)
(913) 273-2552

KENTUCKY
Kentucky Medical Review Organization
10503 Timberwood Circle, Suite 200
P.O. Box 23450
Louisville, KY 40223
1-800-288-1499

LOUISIANA
Louisiana Health Care Review, Inc.
8591 United Plaza Blvd., Suite 270
Baton Rouge, LA 70809
1-800-433-4958 (in-state only)
(504) 926-6353

* PRO will accept collect calls from out of state on this number.

MAINE
Health Care Review, Inc.
(PRO for Maine)
Henry C. Hall Building
345 Blackstone Blvd.
Providence, RI 02906
1-800-541-9888 or 1-800-528-0700
(both numbers in Maine only)
(207) 945-0244*

MARYLAND
Delmarva Foundation for
  Medical Care, Inc.
(PRO for Maryland)
9240 Centreville Road
Easton, MD 21601
1-800-645-0011
In Maryland: 1-800-492-5811

MASSACHUSETTS
Massachusetts Peer Review
  Organization, Inc.
235 Wyman Street
Waltham, MA 02154-1231
1-800-252-5533 (in-state only)
(617) 890-0011*

MICHIGAN
Michigan Peer Review
  Organization
40600 Ann Arbor Road, Suite 200
Plymouth, MI 48170-4495
1-800-365-5899

MINNESOTA
Foundation for Health Care
  Evaluation
Suite 400
2901 Metro Drive
Bloomington, MN 55425
1-800-444-3423

MISSISSIPPI
Mississippi Foundation for
  Medical Care, Inc.
P.O. Box 4665
735 Riverside Drive
Jackson, MS 39296-4665
1-800-844-0600 (in-state only)
(601) 948-8894

* PRO will accept collect calls from out of state on this number.

MISSOURI
Missouri Patient Care Review
 Foundation
505 Hobbs Road, Suite 100
Jefferson City, MO 65109
1-800-347-1016

MONTANA
Montana-Wyoming Founda-
 tion for Medical Care
400 North Park, 2nd Floor
Helena, MT 59601
1-800-497-8232 (in-state
 only)
(406) 433-4020*

NEBRASKA
Iowa Foundation for Medical
 Care/The Sunderbruch
 Corporation
6000 Westown Parkway Suite
350E
West Des Moines, IA 50266
1-800-247-3004 (in-state
 only)
1-800-422-4812 (out-of-state)

NEVADA
Nevada Peer Review
675 East 2100 South, Suite
 270
Salt Lake City, UT 84106-
 1864
1-800-558-0829 (in Nevada
 only)
In Reno: (702) 826-1996
(702) 385-9933*

NEW HAMPSHIRE
New Hampshire Foundation
 for Medical Care
15 Old Rollinsford Road,
 Suite 302
Dover, NH 03820
1-800-582-7174 (in-state
 only)
(603) 749-1641*

NEW JERSEY
The Peer Review Organiza-
 tion of New Jersey, Inc.
Central Division
Brier Hill Court, Building J
East Brunswick, NJ 08816
1-800-624-4557 (in-state
 only)
(201) 238-5570*

* PRO will accept collect calls from out of state on this number.

NEW MEXICO
New Mexico Medical Review Association
707 Broadway N.E., Suite 200
P.O. Box 27449
Albuquerque, NM 87125-7449
1-800-279-6824 (in-state only)
(505) 842-6236
In Albuquerque: 842-6236

NEW YORK
Island Peer Review Organization, Inc.
1979 Marcus Avenue, First Floor
Lake Success, NY 11042
1-800-331-7767 (in-state only)
(516) 326-7767*

NORTH CAROLINA
Medical Review of North Carolina
Suite 203
P.O. Box 37309
5625 Dillard Drive
Cary, NC 27511-9227
1-800-682-2650 (in-state only)
(919) 851-2955

NORTH DAKOTA
North Dakota Health Care Review, Inc.
Suite 301
900 North Broadway
Minot, ND 58701
1-800-472-2902 (in-state only)
(701) 852-4231*

OHIO
Peer Review Systems, Inc.
P.O. Box 6174
757 Brooksedge Plaza Drive
Westerville, OH 43081-6174
1-800-837-0664
1-800-589-7337 (in-state only)

* PRO will accept collect calls from out of state on this number.

OKLAHOMA
Oklahoma Foundation for
  Peer Review, Inc.
Suite 400 The Paragon
  Building
5801 Broadway Extension
Oklahoma City, OK 73118-
  7489
1-800-522-3414 (in-state
  only)
(405) 840-2891

OREGON
Oregon Medical Professional
  Review Organization
Suite 200
1220 Southwest Morrison
Portland, OR 97205
1-800-344-4354 (in-state
  only)
(503) 279-0100*

PENNSYLVANIA
Keystone Peer Review
  Organization, Inc.
777 East Park Drive
P.O. Box 8310
Harrisburg, PA 17105-8310
1-800-322-1914 (in-state
  only)
(717) 564-8288

PUERTO RICO
Puerto Rico Foundation for
  Medical Care
Suite 605 Mercantile Plaza
Hato Rey, PR 00918
(809) 753-6705* or (809)
  753-6708*

RHODE ISLAND
Health Care Review, Inc.
Henry C. Hall Building
345 Blackstone Boulevard
Providence, RI 02906
1-800-221-1691 (New En-
  gland-wide)
In Rhode Island: 1-800-662-
  5028
(401) 331-6661*

SOUTH CAROLINA
Medical Review of North
  Carolina
P.O. Box 37309
Suite 1203
5625 Dillard Drive
Cary, NC 27511-9227
1-800-682-2650 (in-state
  only)
(919) 851-2955

* PRO will accept collect calls from out of state on this number.

SOUTH DAKOTA
South Dakota Foundation for
Medical Care
1323 South Minnesota
Avenue
Sioux Falls, SD 57105
1-800-658-2285

TENNESSEE
Mid-South Foundation for
Medical Care
Suite 400
6401 Poplar Avenue
Memphis, TN 38119
1-800-489-4633

TEXAS
Texas Medical Foundation
Barton Oaks Plaza Two,
Suite 200
901 Mopac Expressway South
Austin, TX 78746
1-800-725-8315 (in-state
only)
(512) 329-6610

UTAH
Utah Peer Review
Organization
675 East 2100 South
Suite 270
Salt Lake City, UT 84106-
1864
1-800-274-2290

VERMONT
New Hampshire Foundation
for Medical Care
(PRO for Vermont)
15 Old Rollinsford Road,
Suite 302
Dover, NH 03820
1-800-772-0151 (in Vermont
only)
(802) 655-6302*

VIRGIN ISLANDS
Virgin Islands Medical Insti-
tute, Inc.
IAD Estate Diamond Ruby
P.O. Box 1566
Christiansted
St. Croix, U.S., VI 00821-
1566
(809) 778-6470*

VIRGINIA
Medical Society of Virginia
Review Organization
1606 Santa Rosa Road,
Suite 200
P.O. Box K 70
Richmond, VA 23288-0070
1-800-545-3814 (DC, MD
and VA)
(804) 289-5320
In Richmond: 289-5397

* PRO will accept collect calls from out of state on this number.

WASHINGTON
(PRO-West)
Suite 100
10700 Meridian Avenue,
   North
Seattle, WA 98133-9075
1-800-445-6941
In Seattle: 368-8272

WEST VIRGINIA
West Virginia Medical Institute, Inc.
3001 Chesterfield Place
Charleston, WV 25304
1-800-642-8686, ext. 266
In Charleston: 346-9864

WISCONSIN
Wisconsin Peer Review Or-
   ganization
2909 Landmark Place
Madison, WI 53713
1-800-362-2320 (in-state
   only)
(608) 274-1940

WYOMING
Montana-Wyoming Founda-
   tion for Medical Care
400 North Park, 2nd Floor
Helena, MT 59601
1-800-497-8232 (in Wyoming
   only)
1-(406) 443-4020*

* PRO will accept collect calls from out of state on this number.

Durable Medical Equipment Regional Carriers

REGION A

Connecticut, Delaware, Maine, Massachusetts, New Hampshire, New Jersey, New York, Pennsylvania, Rhode Island, Vermont

Metra Health Insurance Company
P.O. Box 6800
Wilkes-Barre, PA 18773-6800
1-800-842-2052

REGION B

District of Columbia, Illinois, Indiana, Maryland, Michigan, Minnesota, Ohio, Virginia, West Virginia, Wisconsin
AdminaStar Federal Inc.
P.O. Box 7031
Indianapolis, IN 46207-7031
1-800-270-2313

REGION C

Alabama, Arkansas, Colorado, Florida, Georgia, Kentucky, Louisiana, Mississippi, New Mexico, North Carolina, Oklahoma, South Carolina, Tennessee, Texas, Puerto Rico, Virgin Islands

Palmetto Government Benefits Administrators
Medicare DMERC Operations
P.O. Box 100141
Columbia, SC 29202-0141
1-800-213-5452

REGION D

Alaska, Arizona, California, Hawaii, Idaho, Iowa, Kansas, Missouri, Montana, Nebraska, Nevada, North Dakota, Oregon, South Dakota, Utah, Washington, Wyoming, American Samoa, Marianna Islands, Guam

CIGNA Medicare
P.O. Box 690
Nashville, TN 37202
1-800-899-7095

VETERANS' AFFAIRS OFFICES

UNITED STATES DE-
PARTMENT OF VETER-
ANS AFFAIRS
1 (800) 827-1000

ALABAMA
Alabama Veterans' Affairs De-
partment
770 Washington Ave., Ste 530
Montgomery, AL 36102-1509
Phone: (205) 242-5077
Fax: (205) 242-5102

ALASKA
Alaska Military and Veterans'
Affairs Department
P.O. Box 5800
Fort Richardson, AK 99505-
5800
Phone: (907) 465-4730
Fax: (907) 465-4605

ARIZONA
Arizona Veterans' Service
Commission
3225 North Central Ave., Ste.
910
Phoenix, AZ 85012
Phone: (602) 255-4713
Fax: (602) 255-1038

ARKANSAS
Arkansas Veterans' Affairs De-
partment
P.O. Box 1280
Little Rock, AR 72115
Phone: (501) 370-3820
Fax: (501) 370-3829

CALIFORNIA
California Veterans' Affairs
Department
1227 O. Street
P.O. Box 942895
Sacramento, CA 94295-0001
Phone: (916) 653-2573
Fax: (653)-2456

COLORADO
Colorado Veterans' Affairs Division
Social Services Department
1575 Sherman Street
Denver, CO 80203-1714
Phone: (303) 866-2494
Fax: (303) 866-4214

CONNECTICUT
Connecticut Veterans' Affairs Department
287 West Street
Rocky Hill, CT 06067
Phone: (203) 721-5891
Fax: (203) 721-5904

DISTRICT OF COLUMBIA
Veterans' Affairs Office
Human Services Department
801 North Capitol St., N.E.
Washington, DC 20002
Phone: (202) 727-0328
Fax: (202) 724-4346

FLORIDA
Florida Advisory Commission on Veterans' Affairs
403 Nottingham Ct.
Tallahassee, FL 32579
Phone: (904) 672-8211

GEORGIA
Georgia Veterans' Employment and Training Service
Labor Department
148 International Blvd., N.E.
Atlanta, GA 30303-1751
Phone: (404) 656-3127
Fax: (404) 657-9896
Georgia Veteran's Service Dept.
Floyd Veterans' Memorial Bldg.
Suite E-970
Atlanta, GA 30334
Phone: (404) 656-2300
Fax: (404) 656-7006

GUAM
Guam Veterans' Affairs Office
P.O. Box 3279
Agana, GU 96910
Phone: (671) 472-6002
Fax: (671) 477-4826

HAWAII
Hawaii Veterans' Services Office
Defense Department
3949 Diamond Head Rd.
Honolulu, HI 96816-4495
Phone: (808) 587-3000
Fax: (808) 734-8527

Resources

IDAHO
Idaho State Veterans' Home
320 Collins Rd.
P.O. Box 7765
Boise, ID 83707
Phone: (208) 334-5000

ILLINOIS
Illinois Veterans' Affairs Dept.
833 South Spring Street
P.O. Box 19432
Springfield, IL 62794-9432
Phone: (217) 785-4114
Fax: (217) 524-0344

INDIANA
Indiana Veterans' Education Office
Proprietary Education Commission
302 West Washington St., Rm. E201
Indianapolis, IN 46204
Phone: (317) 232-1320
Fax: (317) 233-4219

Indiana Veterans' Employment and Training Bureau
Welfare Development Department
Indiana Government Ctr. South
10 North Senate Avenue
Indianapolis, IN 46204
Phone: (317) 232-6804
Fax: (317) 233-4793

Indiana Veterans' Affairs Dept.
302 West Washington St., Rm. E120
Indianapolis, IN 46204-2738
Phone: (317) 232-3910
Fax: (317) 232-7721

IOWA
Iowa Veterans' Affairs Com-
mission
Camp Dodge Office Bldg.
7700 N.W. Beaver Dr.
Johnston, IA 50131-1902
Phone: (515) 242-5333
Fax: (515) 242-5659
Iowa Veterans' Home/Veter-
ans' Affairs Commission
1301 Summit St.
Marshaltown, IA 50158
Phone: (515) 752-1501

KANSAS
Kansas Veterans' Affairs Com-
mission
701 Jayhawk Tower
700 S.W. Jackson Street
Topeka, KS 66603
Phone: (913) 296-3976
Fax: (913) 296-1462

LOUISIANA
Louisiana Veterans' Affairs
Commission
P.O. Box 94095
Baton Rouge, LA 70804-
9095
Phone: (504) 922-0500
Fax: (504) 922-0511
Louisiana Veterans Education
and Training Bureau
Education Department
P.O. Box 94064
Baton Rouge, LA 70804-
9064
Phone: (504) 342-3556
Fax: (504) 342-8161

MAINE
Maine Veterans' Services Di-
vision
State House Station #117
Augusta, ME 04333
Phone: (207) 626-4467
Fax: (207) 287-4071

MARYLAND
Maryland Veterans' Commis-
sion
Federal Bldg.
31 Hopkins Plaza, Rm. 110
Baltimore, MD 21201
Phone: (410) 962-4700
Fax: (410) 333-1071

MASSACHUSETTS
Massachusetts Veterans' Ser-
vices Department
100 Cambridge St.
Boston, MA 02202
Phone: (617) 727-3570

MICHIGAN
D.J. Jacobetti Home for Vet-
erans
425 Fisher Street
Marquette, MI 49855
Phone: (906) 226-3576

Grand Rapids Home for Veterans
300 Monroe Avenue, N.W.
Grand Rapids, MI 49505
Phone: (616) 364-5300

Michigan Military and Veterans' Affairs Department
2500 South Washington Avenue
Lansing, MI 48913-5101
Phone: (517) 483-5500
Fax: (517) 483-5822

MINNESOTA
Minnesota Veterans' Affairs
Dept.
Veterans' Service Bldg., 2nd
Fl.
St. Paul, MN 55155
Phone: (612) 296-2562
Fax: (612) 296-3945

MISSISSIPPI
Mississippi Veterans' Affairs
Board
4607 Lindbergh Dr.
Jackson, MS 39209
Phone: (601) 354-7205
Fax: (601) 354-6060

MISSOURI
Missouri Veterans' Commis-
sion
P.O. Drawer 147
Jefferson City, MO 65101
Phone: (314) 751-3779

MONTANA
Montana Veterans' Affairs Di-
vision
Military Affairs Department
P.O. Box 4789
Helena, MT 59604-4789
Phone: (406) 444-6910
Fax: (406) 444-6973

NEBRASKA
Nebraska Veterans' Affairs
Dept.
State Office Bldg.
P.O. Box 95083
Lincoln, NE 68509-5083
Phone: (402) 471-2458

NEVADA
Nevada Veterans' Affairs
Commission
1201 Termal Way, Rm. 108
Reno, NV 89520
Phone: (702) 688-1155
Fax: (702) 688-1656

NEW HAMPSHIRE
New Hampshire Veterans'
Council
359 Lincoln Street
Manchester, NH 03103-4901
Phone: (603) 624-9230

NEW JERSEY
New Jersey Military and Veterans' Affairs Department
101 Eggert Crossing Rd. CN
340
Trenton, NJ 08625-0340
Phone: (609) 530-6892
Fax: (609) 530-7108

NEW MEXICO
New Mexico Veterans' Service Commission
P.O. Box 2324
Santa Fe, MN 87503
Phone: (505) 827-6300

NEW YORK
New York Veterans' Education Bureau
5B28 Cultural Education Ctr.
Albany, NY 12230
Phone: (518) 474-7607
Fax: (518) 468-2175
New York Veterans' Affairs Division
Corning Tower, 28th Fl.
Empire State Plaza
Albany, NY 12223-0001
Phone: (518) 474-3752
Fax: (518) 473-0379

NORTH CAROLINA
North Carolina Veterans' Affairs Division
Administration Department
Albemarle Bldg., Ste. 1065
325 North Salisbury Street.
Raleigh, NC 27603-5940
Phone: (919) 733-3851

NORTH DAKOTA

North Dakota Veterans' Affairs
Department
1411 32nd St. South
P.O. Box 9003
Fargo, ND 58106-9003
Phone: (701) 239-7165
Fax: (701) 239-7166

OKLAHOMA

Oklahoma Veterans' Affairs
Cabinet
Governor's Office
212 State Capitol
Oklahoma City, OK 73105
Phone: (405) 521-3684
Oklahoma Veterans' Affairs
Department
P.O. Box 53067
Oklahoma City, OK 73152
Phone: (405) 521-3684
Fax: (405) 521-6533

OREGON

Oregon Veterans' Employ-
ment Service
Employment Department
875 Union St., N.E.
Salem, OR 97311
Phone: (503) 378-3338
Fax: (503) 373-7298
Oregon Veterans' Affairs De-
partment
700 Summer St., N.E.
Salem, OR 97310
Phone: (503) 373-2000
Fax: (503) 373-2362

PENNSYLVANIA

Pennsylvania Veterans' Em-
ployment and Training Pro-
grams
Labor and Industry Dept.
7th and Forster Streets
Harrisburg, PA 17120
Phone: (717) 787-5835
Fax: (717) 787-5279

RHODE ISLAND

Rhode Island Veterans' Affairs
Division
Human Services Department
Metacom Avenue
Bristol, RI 02809
Phone: (401) 253-8000

SOUTH CAROLINA
South Carolina Veterans' Affairs Division
Governor's Office
Brown State Office Bldg.
1205 Pendleton Street
Columbia, SC 29201
Phone: (803) 734-0200
Fax: (803) 734-0197

SOUTH DAKOTA
South Dakota Military and Veterans' Affairs Department
2823 West Main St.
Rapid City, SD 57702-8186
Phone: (605) 399-6702
Fax: (605) 399-6677

TENNESSEE
Tennessee Veterans' Affairs Department
215 8th Ave. North
Nashville, TN 37243-1010
Phone: (615) 741-6663
Fax: (615) 741-4785

TEXAS
Texas Veterans' Commission
P.O. Box 12277
Austin, TX 78711
Phone: (512) 463-5538
Fax: (512) 475-2395

UTAH
Utah Veterans' Affairs Office
Community and Economic Development Department
324 South State, Suite. 500
Salt Lake City, UT 84111
Phone: (801) 538-8700
Fax: (801) 538-8888

VERMONT
Vermont State Veterans' Affairs Office
120 State Street
Montpelier, VT 05620-4401
Phone: (802) 828-3380

VIRGIN ISLANDS
Virgin Islands Veterans' Affairs Bureau
22-21 Kongens Gade
St. Thomas, VI 00802
Phone: (809) 773-6663

VIRGINIA
Virginia Veterans' Affairs Department
210 Franklin Rd., S.W.
Roanoke, VA 24011
Phone: (703) 857-7104
Fax: (703) 857-7573

WASHINGTON
Washington Veterans' Affairs
Department
505 East Union
P.O. Box 41150
Olympia, WA 98504-1150
Phone: (206) 753-4522
Fax: (206) 586-5540

WEST VIRGINIA
West Virginia Veterans' Affairs
Division
Military Affairs and Public
Safety Department
1321 Plaza East, Suite 101
Charleston, WV 25301-1400
Phone: (304) 558-3662

WISCONSIN
Wisconsin Veterans' Affairs
Department
P.O. Box 7843
Madison, WI 53707
Phone: (608) 266-1311
Fax: (608) 267-0403

WYOMING
Wyoming Veterans' Affairs
Council
Herschler Bldg., 2nd Fl. East
122 West 25th Street
Cheyenne, WY 82002
Phone: (307) 632-8389

MISCELLANEOUS RESOURCES

ALZHEIMER'S ASSOCIATION
1 (800) 272-3900
Through local chapters and monthly newsletters, this organization offers public education programs and support services to patients and families who are coping with Alzheimer's disease. The twenty-four-hour, toll-free hotline links families with nearby chapters which are familiar with local resources and can offer practical suggestions for daily living.

AMERICAN DIABETES ASSOCIATION
1 (800) 232-3472
(703) 549-1500
Local chapters of the Association offer patients and families educational materials, support, and referral to appropriate community resources. A publications list is available to the public on request.

AMERICAN HEART ASSOCIATION
(214) 748-7212
The American Heart Association sponsors public education programs through local chapters where patients and families exchange practical advice for recovering from stroke. A list of publications is available from local chapters.

AMERICAN LUNG ASSOCIATION
(212) 315-8700
The American Lung Association conducts public and professional education programs on preventing, detecting, and treating lung diseases and on living with disabled breathing. Local chapters distribute a variety of publications and self-help guides.

AMERICAN PARKINSON'S DISEASE ASSOCIATION
1 (800) 223-2732
(212) 685-2741
The American Parkinson's Disease Association educates the public about this disease and offers assistance to patients and their families. The toll-free hotline will refer callers to local chapters that provide information on community services. A list of publications is available upon request.

CHOICE IN DYING, INC.
1 (800) 989-WILL
For information on advance directives and copies of state Durable Powers of Attorney for Health Care (Health Care Proxy) forms and living wills. Choice in Dying also provides counseling to families and maintains a living will registry. Choice in Dying has numerous available publications written for the general public as well as more technical information for professionals.

CONSUMER INFORMATION CENTER
P.O. Box 100
Pueblo, CO 81009
The Consumer Information Center, a program of the General Services Administration, helps federal government agencies promote and distribute useful information to the general public. The Consumer Information Catalogue is available upon request.

DISABLED AMERICAN VETERANS
(513) 684-2676
Disabled American Veterans is a private, nonprofit organization that represents veterans with service-connected disabilities and their families. A list of free publications is available from DAV service offices located in each state.

HELP FOR INCONTINENT PEOPLE
(803) 579-7900
Help for Incontinent People is a patient advocacy group that works to educate the public about the prevalence, diagnosis, and treatment of urinary incontinence. A publications list is available upon request.

HUNTINGTON'S DISEASE SOCIETY OF AMERICA
1 (800) 345-4372
The Society conducts a hotline which offers crisis intervention, genetic counseling, and referral services. The Society also sponsors self-help groups around the country and publishes a quarterly newsletter and pamphlets on a variety of topics.

NATIONAL AIDS INFORMATION CLEARINGHOUSE
For publication orders: 1 (800) 458-5231
AIDS hotline: 1 (800) 342-2437
Spanish-speaking hotline: 1 (800) 344-SIDA

NATIONAL ARTHRITIS AND MUSCULOSKELETAL AND SKIN DISEASES INFORMATION CLEARING-HOUSE
(301) 496-8188
The Clearinghouse helps the public locate up-to-date information about arthritis, musculoskeletal disorders, and skin diseases. Free catalogues are available from the Clearinghouse upon request.

NATIONAL DIGESTIVE DISEASES INFORMATION CLEARINGHOUSE
(301) 654-3810
The Clearinghouse offers information about digestive diseases to health professionals and the general public.

NATIONAL HOSPICE ASSOCIATION
(703) 243-5900
The National Hospice Association promotes quality care for terminally ill patients and provides information on hospice services in the United States.

NATIONAL INFORMATION CENTER ON DEAFNESS
1 (800) 672-6720
The National Information Center on Deafness distributes information on deafness to the general public. A list of publications is available.

NATIONAL KIDNEY AND UROLOGIC INFORMATION CLEARINGHOUSE
(301) 654-4415
The Clearinghouse offers information about kidney diseases to the general public. Free publications are available upon request.

NATIONAL MULTIPLE SCLEROSIS SOCIETY
1 (800) 624-8236
The Society organizes local chapters around the country and publishes materials that are available upon request.

NATIONAL ASSOCIATION OF PROFESSIONAL GERIATRIC CARE MANAGERS
(602) 881-8008
Professional Care Managers are social workers, nurses, psychologists, and other trained professionals in private practice who are available to assess individual care needs and obtain the help that is needed. Professional care managers are located throughout the country and are often involved managing the care of a frail or disabled person if family members are not available to do so.

NATIONAL ACADEMY OF ELDERLAW ATTORNEYS
1604 North Country Club Road
Tucson, AZ 85716
This national organization sets national standards for the delivery of elder law; its members can be found in all states where they specialize in serving the elderly and assisting them with lifetime planning. For information, send a self-addressed. stamped envelope to the above address and ask for "How to Select an Elder Law Attorney."

NATIONAL ELDERCARE LOCATOR
1 (800) 677-1116
This consumer help line is available for information on the extensive network of state and local resources for the aged and their families: home delivered meals, transportation, legal assistance, housing, home health care, adult day care, and more.

NATIONAL CITIZENS COALITION FOR NURSING HOME REFORM
(202) 393-2018

OLDER WOMEN'S LEAGUE
(202) 783-6686
Local OWL chapters offer mutual aid and supportive services. OWL publishes a monthly newsletter and issues other publications that are available upon request.

SOCIAL SECURITY ADMINISTRATION
1 (800) 772-1213
To obtain general information on Old Age benefits, Supplemental Security Income benefits, and Disability benefits; and to obtain the addresses and telephone numbers of local Social Security Administration District Offices. The Social Security Administration has numerous explanatory publications available to the general public.

WELL SPOUSE FOUNDATION
1-800-383-0879
This self-help group is a resource for well spouses who are taking care of a disabled spouse. The group has a newsletter and organizes meetings and conferences in which well spouses can get together to develop local support groups.

Index

Geriatric care managers, 231–32

Grantor of trust, 211

Grouping of residents in nursing homes, 187

Guaranteed renewable Medigap policy, 129

Guardianship, 226–29

H

Health-related facilities (HRFs), 174–75

Health care benefits for veterans, *see* Veterans' benefits

Health insurance, employee, loss of, 142–44

Health maintenance organizations (HMOs)
  Medicaid, 121
  Medicare, 133–35, 138

Home and community-based waiver programs, Medicaid, 164

Home care
  applying for services, 157
  availability, variations in, 155
  certified agencies, 155–56, 161–62, 163
  costs, 157–58
  employee health insurance plans, 165
  employment contracts with workers and agencies, 166
  enforcing rights, 166–67

home health aide services, 153

hospice programs, 156–57

housekeeper/chore services, 154

Medicaid coverage
  applying for services, 164
  eligibility generally, 162–63
  home and community-based waiver programs, 164
  mandatory and optional services, 163–64
  medical services, 163
  personal care services, 164
  skilled home health services, 163

medical services, 152–53

Medicare, 94–95

Medicare coverage
  appealing a denial, 162
  applying for coverage, 161
  co-payments, 161
  deductibles, 161
  eligibility rules, 159–60
  prior hospitalization not required, 161
  services covered, 160

Medigap plans, 165–66

miscellaneous services, 154

Index